# A MOTHER'S SEARCH FOR HOPE

# GOODBYE FOREVER?

## JOY SWIFT

REVIEW AND HERALD® PUBLIS
HAGERSTOWN, M

Copyright 2002 by
Review and Herald® Publishing Association
All rights reserved

This book was
Edited by Gerald Wheeler
Cover designed by Mark O'Conner
Interior designed by Tina M. Ivany
Electronic makeup by Tina M. Ivany
Cover art by PhotoDisc
Typeset: Bembo 11/13

PRINTED IN U.S.A.

06  05  04  03  02          5  4  3  2  1

**R&H Cataloging Service**
Swift, Joy, 1957–
    Goodbye forever?

    1. Swift, Joy, 1957–    2. Mass murder—United States—Case
Studies.    3. Death.

236.1

ISBN 0-8280-1539-2

To order additional copies of *Goodbye Forever?* by Joy Swift,
call 1-800-765-6955.
Visit us at www.reviewandherald.com for information on
other Review and Herald® products.

# C O N T E N T S

# ONE

# TRAGEDY

The box from Grandma Swift arrived just after noon, and the girls and I tore into it as if it was Christmas. It contained secondhand clothes from the cousins for our three older children. It also had bicentennial bell banks for the two little ones, and a globe we'd been wanting to help the boys with their geography lessons.

But most precious of all was a 5" x 7" framed photograph of the whole family taken at a family reunion when Stacy was only two months old. My husband's aunt had insisted we pose for a family portrait before we went home. Now I admired the smiling faces of our children surrounding George and me, with his mother beside us. "A fine-looking family," I said to myself as I propped the picture up on the television set. I wanted it to be the first thing George and the boys saw when they came home tonight from work and school.

Three-year-old Tonya skipped about our Ozarks home ringing her liberty bell with glee. Stacy, now 17 months, tried her best to keep up with her sister. I busied myself sorting the clothes into piles. The boys, Steve, 14, and Greg, 12, would have to try on some of the jeans. Greg would be home right after school, but Steve would pop in only a few minutes to change clothes before heading to his after-school job at the Sportsman Resort.

I didn't know when Stephanie, 17, would try on hers, though. It had been four weeks since the doctors had diagnosed her with ovarian cancer. She was now in a hospital 100 miles away undergoing treatment. The doctors had given us little hope for her survival, but we were determined to prove them wrong. They had allowed her to come home the previous weekend, which had lifted her spirits considerably. She had been in a great deal of pain, though, and we had had to take her back early. George had gone to see her the night before, and she seemed to be feeling better. If all went well she might be allowed to visit again this coming weekend.

The school bus pulled to a stop out front, and Tonya and Stacy couldn't wait to meet their brothers at the door. They tackled Greg as he entered, and he threw himself on the floor to tickle the girls. After being the youngest for so long, he relished his big brother role.

Steve had to rush to change into work clothes if he was to catch the bus on its way off the peninsula and get a free ride to work. But I did make sure he saw the family portrait and pile of clothes before he dashed out the door.

I was relieved to see that Billy Dyer had not gotten off the bus with Greg. George and I both felt that Greg spent too much time with the boy. There was something about him that we didn't quite trust, and we preferred that if they did spent time together that they play at our house where we could keep an eye on them.

More than anything else we wished that Greg would tire of Billy's pranks and find a new friend.

George came home early, and I was so excited about the package that I ran out to meet him. He, too, had quite a story to tell. The town had held a big bass tournament so he had finished painting the local American Legion Post building as quickly as possible and then went over to watch. There he got involved in launching boats and weighing fish, soaking his 14-year-old kangaroo hide boots clear through. Someday, he vowed, he would compete in a bass tournament himself.

Once inside George called Greg, who came running and wrestled with him for a few moments.

"Greg, I want you to take the laces out of my boots and run 'em over to the dump," his father said.

I was in shock, having assumed that he'd never throw those old friends away. I figured they'd have to hang over the mantel or some other privileged spot for the rest of his life. Nope, he had decided to give the boots a decent burial after all those years of faithful service. So Greg took out the laces and ran the boots across the road to the dump.

An hour later I drove to the store to get something for dinner. The check-out girl asked if we planned to play Bingo at the American Legion that night. I hadn't even thought about it being Thursday night. We hadn't gone since Stephanie had been in the hospital.

During dinner I reminded the boys that they would have school pictures taken the next day and to pick out a nice shirt to wear.

"I'm just going to wear this one," Steve said, pointing to his favorite green T-shirt that he had on.

I hinted that he might find something nicer in his pile of clothes. But I waited until after dinner to remind George that it was Thursday night and to ask if he wanted to play Bingo that night.

"I'll think about it," he said.

As I went in to clean the kitchen George called the boys to his side and asked if they'd mind watching the girls so we could go out.

"Aw, Dad, you guys always get to go out," Steve complained.

"Now, Steve," his father replied, "we haven't been out in a long time. And besides, we let you guys go to the movies Tuesday. Don't you think it's our turn?"

They argued back and forth, and I stopped to listen to their playful bickering. In the end, their dad won. They really didn't mind watching the girls but just weren't going to pass up an opportunity for a good argument. I loved to listen to them, each one trying to outdo the other. Then, with hugs and kisses, we started on our way.

It was quite a bit colder than I expected, so I ran back in to get a sweater while George continued toward the car. Stacy wrestled me for the door as I tried to leave. She wanted her "Baaa-Baa." I called for Greg and asked him to fix her a bottle of juice.

He jumped right up and headed for the refrigerator, grabbing the bottle from Stacy on the way. At 17 months Stacy was still very attached to her bottle. It was her security, and I hadn't had the heart to wean her from it yet.

Tonya was rocking on the bed beside the door. I bent down to give her one last kiss and told her to be good for the boys. "Steve, take good care of the girls for me," I said before going out the door.

"I will," he said, not even glancing up from the TV. Then I was out the door, ready for a nice evening away from home.

It surprised me that George was sitting in the passenger seat when I came out because he rarely wanted me to drive when we went anywhere. As much as he likes chili, his stomach doesn't necessarily thank him for eating it.

It was dark and foggy, and I had to drive a little slower than usual. We stopped at Poor Jim's Restaurant to see if our friends Steven and Mary were about ready to close so they could join us. Steven had just finished cooking the last dinner, and he and George went outside for a cigarette. Mary and I cleaned tables, waiting for the last table of customers to finish eating. They ate leisurely. George and I finally decided to go on and promised to save them a seat.

When we reached the Legion Post, George picked out our Bingo cards while I went over to talk to the auxiliary president. I apologized for missing the meeting the night before, explaining that my husband had gone to the hospital to see Stephanie, leaving me in charge of the other kids. I had really wanted to go, but something inside me had told me not to leave the kids the previous night. It was a feeling I could not explain. But tonight, with George beside me, I felt completely at ease.

Finding some seats in the middle of the crowd, we laid out our cards and Bingo markers, ready to play. Steven and Mary arrived in the middle of the first game, and we motioned them to our table. None of us won a single thing, but we were having fun.

Around 10:00, in the middle of a game, someone I didn't know called George outside. A few minutes later my husband signaled for me to come too. He looked very upset. Outside was total pandemonium as more than a dozen people talked at once. I couldn't understand anything they said. The man who had summoned George was crying. I heard my husband ask him what had happened.

"Just go home," he cried. "Something terrible. Please, just go home."

I was totally confused. Someone referred to the crying man as Pete. George headed for the car. Wanting to know what was going on, I yelled, "Pete, what happened?"

"Please, just go home," he repeated as he turned away. I ran for the car. As I caught up with my husband I heard someone ask Steven and Mary if they were our friends. "You'd better go with them," the person said. "They're going to need you."

We jumped into the car and sped for home.

That first 10 miles was the longest in my life. We didn't talk at all. George kept his eyes fixed on the road ahead. A million tragedies ran through my mind. One of the kids must be hurt. Steph must have taken a bad turn and needed us right away. The water heater blew up and set the house on fire. The drive took forever.

Three miles before home we looked across the lake to where our house stood on a hill. Usually we could see the yard lamp glowing through the trees, but tonight flashing red lights covered the whole hill. The police had a roadblock set up just before our house, checking all vehicles coming and going. Half panicked now, we told the officer who we were. He let us through. Police cars and ambulances lined the road in front of our house. George slammed on the brakes, jumped out, and raced for the front door. I ran around the back of the car to avoid the roadside ditch. Halfway across the yard two ambulance attendants, a man and a woman, grabbed me by the arms.

"Let me go!" I yelled. "Those are my kids in there. I've got to get in there!"

They held on tightly and pulled me across the road to an ambulance. Sitting me down on the bumper, they stood in front of me like guards, just in case I tried to run for the house. Shaking uncontrollably, I tried to calm down. Glancing toward the house, I saw that George had made it to the porch before two officers stopped him. It was obvious they weren't going to let him in either.

Trying hard to show an air of self-control, I looked up at the woman. "What happened?" My eyes pleaded for an answer.

"We don't know," she said quietly.

Again I looked toward the house. "Where are my kids? Are they in the ambulance?" I spun around, wanting desperately to see them there. Instead I saw only white emptiness. I turned back to the woman, my teary eyes begging for an answer.

"They're still in the house," the woman stammered.

Again I stared at the house. It was pitch black! Nobody was in there trying to help my kids. If they were hurt, they wouldn't just leave them in there alone. If they were OK, why didn't they let my kids come out to me? I could think of only one rational explanation. Turning to the attendants and in almost a whisper I said, "They're all dead, aren't they?"

The two EMTs bowed their heads, afraid to look at me. "Yes," the woman sighed.

Suddenly I felt totally empty inside and wept silently. Seeing George coming toward me, I met him in the middle of the road. We stood there hugging each other as tightly as we could. Just then Steven and Mary drove up, and Mary ran to me and grabbed me. "Oh, Joy, I'm sorry, so sorry," she cried.

The four of us stood in the middle of the road for a long time.

The police told us only that someone had entered the house and shot all of the kids. They gave no other details. Unable to comprehend how anyone could do that, I began to say crazy things. "Why didn't they go next door? Nobody was home there. Why didn't they just steal everything we had? They could have had it all. I don't want it. Why didn't they tie the kids up and lock them in a closet? Why didn't they kidnap them? At least then I could get them back. Why did they have to kill them? They didn't gain anything by that!

Nobody gained anything by killing them! Why did they have to kill them?"

Then burying my face in George's chest, I cried. Steven yelled to the police for someone to get Don Turner, the Baptist minister who held services in the summer church next door as well. We were not Baptists. For that matter, we hadn't gone to any church in our entire married lives. But when Don Turner learned of Stephanie's illness and the financial hardships it had created, he had brought over a box of canned goods and a check to help us out.

Pastor Turner arrived immediately and stood beside us in the road in front of the house. A short time later an officer walked over to ask if we would come to the police station, but I adamantly refused.

"I'm not leaving here till you bring my kids out. I'm staying right here." I stood firm. "I will not leave them."

It didn't matter to me how much time passed. I had no place else to go.

In desperation the officer asked Don to try to persuade us to go. Again I refused.

"There are relatives who need to be notified," Don said quietly. "We need to get their phone numbers and addresses."

Immediately my mind focused on all the relatives that had to be told. I was ready to go. But first they had to promise me they'd bring me right back as soon as we made the calls. The officer shook his head half-heartedly.

Steven offered his restaurant as a base to phone

the relatives, and I quickly agreed. I felt much better going to a familiar place and was sure I had a better chance of getting back to the house more quickly. Don offered to drive us in his car with Steven and Mary leading in theirs.

When we reached the restaurant I walked briskly inside with Mary and started asking all the whys all over again.

Don Turner came in and grabbed me by the shoulders, spinning me around and looking me square in the eye. "Joy, you've got to be strong now. We need you. George has just broken down outside. He's in the parking lot throwing up."

"I gotta go to him," I said, struggling to escape his grasp.

Holding me tighter, he pulled me back. "No," he said. "Steven is with him. We need you to give us the addresses of the people you want to contact. We'll find a minister to go to their homes. This is not something you tell someone over the phone."

Immediately I stood up straight. "I'm bigger than this. I'm not going to be stupid and lose my head. I can be strong! I must rise above this." Then I gave Don the addresses of the closest relatives. He made the necessary calls to send ministers with the horrible news.

George came in looking very pale and drained. We sat together and waited. When I felt I could stand it no longer I told Don I was ready to return to the house. He put me off, telling me to wait a bit more.

Finally a police officer arrived and put us into a patrol car with no more of an explanation than "Let's go."

Don, Steven, and Mary followed in their cars. I was relieved to be heading back to the house. George and I sat in the back seat almost afraid to let go of each other. If I had stayed with him at the restaurant I would have been by his side when he broke down. Now I didn't want to leave him again. We drove 10 miles before passing our road. Leaning over the seat, I informed the officer that he'd missed the turn. He paused for a minute.

"I was told to take you to the police station first," he finally replied.

Suddenly I felt lied to. I'd been deceived. And I hurt so badly inside. If someone had hollered down my throat just then it would have echoed right back at them.

It was after midnight when we reached the police station. They escorted us into a front office with a big glass wall looking out to the main entry hall. Steven, Mary, and Don stayed with me. A police officer took George to another area for questioning. He was gone four hours. As I waited, my rage and anger began to boil. I asked Don why I couldn't find the ones who did this to my kids and string them up and shoot them a thousand times. Didn't the Bible say, "An eye for an eye"? I wanted to kill them as they had killed my babies. My kids had never hurt anybody.

Pastor Turner listened to my angry words for a long time. He spoke calmly and quietly, but nothing he said made sense to me. Nor could he quote me anything from the Bible to justify my children's deaths. I was full of questions, and I wasn't getting any answers. Don told me that I should feel sorry for the ones who did this.

Sorry? How could I feel sorry for the ones who had murdered my babies? "They're murderers," I yelled. "What could my kids have possibly done to provoke anyone to kill them?"

When my father called, the pastor handed the phone to me. "Honey, what happened?" my dad asked in disbelief.

"Dad, somebody broke into the house and shot the kids. They're all dead!"

"Do you want Mom and me to come down? Do you need us?"

"I don't know, Dad," I said, bursting into tears. "It's OK if you want to come, but there isn't much we can do now."

He said they'd leave right away. They didn't even pack a suitcase.

George joined us around 4:00 a.m. and just as quickly an officer came for me. I don't remember all the questions during those three hours. But he asked if anyone had been over to the house during the last few days. Just Billy Dyer, the 14-year-old neighbor boy who played with our son Greg, though I could not for the moment remember his last name. There had been no sales people, no strangers. Just Billy. I told him about the play fight the boys had had with George just before we left. Looking concerned, the officer asked if my husband had beaten the boys. I had to laugh. George never punished those kids! I was the one who had to dish out the discipline. Their father never even spanked them.

The officer checked the tread on my shoes. They had found prints outside a window through which the killer or killers apparently had fled. I told him about George's boots, how Greg had thrown them away, and where the dump was in case they needed to find them. The questions continued.

In another room the police tested my hands to see whether I had fired a gun in the past 24 hours. After a woman took me into a restroom and strip-searched me, the questions resumed. How many guns did George have?

Later I learned that they had actually suspected George as the killer. They fingerprinted him, strip-searched him, and took pictures of him. And they even took his shirt because it had a chili stain on it. They thought it might be blood. He had a huge bruise on his leg from a boat that had slipped during launching that day, but the police wondered if perhaps he'd sustained it in a scuffle with the kids.

The officer questioned me about George and Steven Pyeatt. When they had gone outside for a cigarette at the restaurant that evening did they have time to go to the house and return? Our house was some 13 miles away. And besides, it was not unusual for Steven to go out between meals. He didn't like to smoke in the kitchen. Having nothing to hide, I was cooperative during the questioning. I wanted to help them find the killers. But it wasn't George. Later it would amaze me how many times Billy Dyer's name came up during the questioning.

I was taken back to the glass office where I found my parents talking with Don and George. Feeling that she might need it, I went over and gave my mom a hug. When I looked at a watch I discovered it was 7:30 Friday morning. We had spent the whole night at the police station. I was still waiting for someone to return me to the house. So far, in all that questioning, I still hadn't gotten any answers.

Mom announced that she wanted to go to the clinic to get something to calm her down and suggested that I accompany her. I told her I couldn't—that I had to stay until I found out what had happened to my kids. Mom begged me again and again to accompany her to the clinic. I stubbornly refused, but as she kept on, I threw my husband a "help, get her off my back" look.

"Just go," he said. "They'll bring you right back."

So much for support! If Mom needed something to calm her down, fine. But I didn't need any drugs to keep me strong.

"She needs you," George whispered. "Just go on."

Finally I agreed. Don volunteered to drive us. The minute we walked outside into the bright morning sun the school buses went by.

"Oh God, the buses," I whimpered.

Today was Friday: school picture day. My boys wouldn't be there. Nor would they ever ride that bus again. The kids were dead, and the whole world just went about its business. People were going to work, children were going to school. Couldn't they feel how badly I hurt inside? Why did they continue as if nothing had happened? The whole world should mourn the loss of my babies!

Don took my arm and led me to the car. A nurse met us at the back door of the clinic. She recognized me but couldn't place who I was. I told her I had brought Stephanie in a few weeks before and that she had ovarian cancer. The nurse thought that was the reason we had come. But when I told her what had really happened she ran crying from the room. Minutes later she returned with the doctor.

He calmly prepared a hypodermic and turned to me.

"Oh no," I said, "I'm fine. Mom's the one who wants the shot."

"It's just to calm you down," he said.

"I don't need to calm down. I'm calm. I have to find out what happened to my kids. I've got to know how they were killed."

They all tried to convince me it would be easier for me if I just took the sedative.

"It won't put me to sleep, will it? I can't go to sleep. I've got to get back to the house."

They promised me it wouldn't put me to sleep.

"All right, all right, just do it so I can get back," I demanded.

"Do you want that in your arm or your hip?" the doctor asked.

"In my arm. It's faster." I didn't have time to half undress for the stupid thing. When he finished, I turned to Mom. "It's your turn."

"Oh, I don't need anything," she answered.

I wanted to hit her. My own mother had deceived me. It seemed as if everybody was lying to me. I was fine. I was as strong or stronger than the rest of them. I hadn't needed that shot!

I did not realize at that time what had been happening behind my back. Don Turner had spent five anguishing hours at the police station listening to my angry words and demands that someone return me to the house. Unable to calm me down, he became alarmed at my behavior and phoned the local clinic for advice. The doctor told him to bring me in for a tranquilizer that would force me to rest.

The minister asked my mother if she thought I would go willingly. Knowing how stubborn I can be, she told him she was sure that I would not. Pretending to need a sedative was not just her doing, but an effort on the part of several people to help me at this critical time. Their plan worked, though for years without a word of complaint my mother took the blame for deceiving me.

Mom would probably have accepted a sedative herself, but at the time nobody knew who had killed the children or whether the murderer might come after George and me next. When my parents and Pastor Turner became aware of this, they agreed that Mom needed to be alert in order to protect us.

We were taken back to the station and returned to the glass office that I had come to think of as the monkey cage. Everybody that entered the station could see us. I felt as if we were on display.

Dad was pacing the floor when suddenly he broke down and started to cry. He tried desperately to stop, but the tears defied him and refused to quit. My husband went over and put his arm around his shoulder.

"I'm sorry, George," Dad cried, disgusted with himself. "I came down here to be strong for you, and now I'm crying like a baby."

"Hey, we're all going to cry," George comforted. "That's why we're all here. To give each other support when one of us breaks down. Don't be sorry for it."

The injection was trying to put me to sleep, and I fought it with everything I had. The room was spinning, and I couldn't see straight. It was difficult to sit up in the straight metal chairs. Walking over to the desk, I sat in the padded chair, resting my head to try to gain some control over the drug. I refused to let it put me to sleep.

While I sat at the desk, several reporters from Springfield filed into the main hall with their microphones and cameras. They looked at us in the monkey cage but had no idea who we were.

A deputy came out of an office to answer questions. I stood and pressed close against the glass to hear. The deputy told the reporters that the younger boy had been found in the yard, apparently running away from the house when he had been gunned down.

"They found Greg outside in the yard!" I cried, turning to George.

The older boy had been found under a couch, the deputy continued, and one of the girls had been in a bed. The other girl had been on the floor.

I was mad! This deputy was telling reporters—

strangers—about my kids, and he hadn't even had the decency to notify us first.

One of the reporters asked how old the children were. The deputy hesitated before answering. He thought the boys were 12 and 14, which was correct. Then he said that the girls appeared to be "1 and—I don't know—2, maybe."

I blew up. Tonya would have been 4 years old in 11 days. Pounding my fist against the glass, I screamed, "She's 4! She's 4!"

All the reporters turned and looked at me. Dad and George pulled me away from the glass. Just then one of the cameramen took a shot of me. I saw it later on the news. I really did have control of myself. I just wanted to let them know I was mad. Finally I calmed down so Dad and George would let me go of me. I wouldn't have gotten angry if everybody had treated me fairly. There were things I needed to do and nobody would listen.

The interview ended and the deputy ducked back into another office. I sat down at the desk again. The sedative was getting harder to fight. More than an hour later the deputy finally came in to talk to us. As he walked up to the desk I grabbed him by the collar and shook him. "How dare you tell those reporters about my kids before you tell me! We've been here all night. I've answered all your questions, and you haven't told me a thing!" My blood boiled.

Again George pulled me away. Lied to, deceived, and treated as if I had no feelings at all, I had to take it out on someone. Tired of trying to be civil about it, I had to let them know how I felt. I had to demand my rights. But I was still under control. I knew what my limits were. I didn't want to hurt anybody—except the killers, of course. But only with permission. I didn't want to go to prison for killing that scum.

The deputy fixed his collar, apologized, and repeated what he had told the reporters. He informed us that the house was sealed until the investigation squad from Jefferson City was through.

Why hadn't they told me that before? I hadn't even thought of the need to collect evidence. If they had leveled with me on that I would have cooperated. Now I understood why I wasn't allowed to go into my own house that night.

# THE MOTEL

The police arranged for us two adjoining rooms at a nearby motel, one for George and me and the other for my parents. They also told us not to leave town until notified. We drove to the motel in Dad's car, stopping to get a Springfield newspaper along the way. The headline read: "Four Camden County Children Found Slain."

Not until I saw the details in print did the reality of it hit me. Here on the front page for all to see was a story about my children. The article indicated that the police had found Stacy on the floor next to a bedroom. She had been drinking from her bottle when killed—the bottle I had asked Greg to fix for her as I headed out the door that night.

All the children had been fully clothed and had not been bound. The paper said that the police found no sign of forcible entry and that the children might have known their attackers. A girl who had sometimes baby-sat for us had come to our house to deliver a message and discovered the children dead, then called the police. Later we learned that it had been Debbie Balentine, a friend of Stephanie's who had come to tell us that our daughter was being allowed to come home from the hospital for the weekend. Steph had called her because we had no phone. We were thankful Debbie had not been caught in the gunfire.

The article was far from accurate, though, with incorrect names, ages, and other facts. We wondered how many other details were wrong as we did our best to piece together what had happened in the house that night. Also we kept the television on to catch any news that the authorities might release.

Don Turner and two police officers visited the motel later that morning. They needed someone to identify the bodies at the morgue. Quickly I volunteered. At last I could see my babies! After some argument Dad went instead. Why couldn't anybody understand how much I needed to be with my kids? Going to the other room, I cried alone.

By the time my father returned the sedative was taking effect. I lay down and fell into a deep sleep. While I slept George and Dad went to a clothing store and bought us each a new outfit. With the house sealed by the investigation squad we couldn't get any of our clothes. None of us had any other clothes except what was on our backs, and George didn't even have a shirt since the police had taken it to examine a stain on it. Earlier the ambulance attendant had loaned me a jacket at the house, because I was shaking so badly. After the police confiscated George's shirt I gave him the jacket to cover up his bare chest. When Don told the clerk at the store the situation, Dad was able to buy the outfits at a reduced rate.

I awoke many hours later to the sound of voices in Mom and Dad's room. Mom showed me the clothes they'd purchased, noting that the clerk at the store had even taken the pants up for me. I'm only five foot two, and pants are always too long when I buy them. Mom is also the same height, so she knew how much they needed to be altered.

It surprised me that I had slept so soundly. Always the last one in the family to fall asleep, I could not relax until I knew all the children were sleeping peacefully in their beds. It was not unusual for me to still be wide awake at 3:00 when the baby cried or one of the kids coughed in the night. That sedative the doctor gave me must have been really strong!

As we talked, Don brought up the question of what to do once the authorities released the house. He suggested that we assign power of attorney to a trusted friend to remove our belongings from it and store them until we found another place to live. We decided to ask Bob and Doris Lading, the president and vice president of the American Legion Post, since they could enlist the help of the entire American Legion membership. We phoned them, and they agreed to come to the motel to discuss the details. Don obtained an attorney to type up the necessary papers.

Deputy Vaughn and another officer arrived at the motel looking very tired. Neither had slept all night Thursday nor all day Friday. It would be 36 hours before they would be able to go home! The deputy told us that they had gone to the junior high school Friday morning to meet with two boys who had information about a juvenile who had bragged during the past two weeks of planning to kill our kids. The police went to the juvenile's home a few miles from our house and took him into custody, along with a 20-year-old man named Ray Richardson. George and I didn't know any Ray Richardson. The police wouldn't tell us who the juvenile was. Legally they couldn't. We questioned them right and left, but they were sworn to silence. They didn't want to do anything to mess up the case.

As the officers stood to leave, one turned to me and asked, "By the way—Billy—was his last name Dyer or Dryer or—"

"It's Dyer," I said, remembering at last. "That's it."

"OK," he replied and turned back toward the door.

"He's the one," George accused. "He's the one that killed them, isn't he?"

"We don't know that," the officer stammered. "We're questioning him, but we don't know."

"He did it," George persisted.

Shortly after the officers left another news program came on. We sat inches from the screen watching ambulance litters being carried from the house. Steve's sneakered foot dangled from under the sheet that covered him. Tonya and Stacy had been placed together on the same litter and covered by a single sheet. Although we were starving for more answers, the news left us unsatisfied. Too many pieces were still missing.

Around 11:00 we all went to bed. It was strange simply to undress and climb into bed. Bedtime had been so much more complex with the kids. After a drink and potty run and Stacy's diaper had been changed, they all had to be tucked in. There was often that last minute "hey, Dad," to throw in one more word before the lights went out. We always checked each one again before we went to bed. Now I suddenly felt unneeded and worthless. And I had not eaten all day without even realizing it.

Saturday morning Pastor Turner informed us that the investigation team had finished their work and released the house if we needed anything from it. Again, I was not allowed to go. It didn't matter now, though. The kids were no longer there. I didn't care if I ever saw the house again, and I never did. I gave Mom and Dad descriptions of the clothes I wanted.

My parents left with Don, leaving George and me to read the three newspapers the pastor had brought with him. Our story was on the front page of each one. They contradicted each other so much that it was difficult to decide which one to believe.

The Springfield *News and Leader* read: "Slaying of Children Stuns Area Residents." A picture of two officers investigating evidence inside the house accompanied a copy of my new family portrait. I had no idea, when I had received it in the mail, that it would be on the front page of a newspaper the next day.

The headline of the St. Louis *Globe-Democrat* declared: "Two Questioned in Killing of Four Children." We learned that two guns were missing from the house and probably had been used to kill the kids. This hurt George deeply. Only the .22 pistol had been loaded, and it had only two bullets in it as far as he knew.

The Kansas City *Times* was the most detailed of all. Its headline announced: "Lake Area Baffled by

Slayings of Four Children." Below the headline were pictures of each of the kids, apparently taken from my wallet at the house. It said the police had no witnesses, no motive, and no weapon.

We needed to sign the power of attorney papers to let others take care of our possessions for us. Don Turner offered to drive George and me to the attorney's office because we still did not have our cars. On the way we passed the police station and noticed Billy Dyer's stepfather's truck parked outside.

"That's Billy's truck," George said.

"It is," I confirmed.

George turned to Don. "He did it. He killed the kids."

"Now we don't know that," the minister stammered. "Maybe Billy just knows something about it. Maybe he can help."

George shook his head. "No, he did it. I know he did."

Don was silent the rest of the way.

At the attorney's office we signed the papers allowing Bob and Doris Lading to take our personal belongings from the house and store them until we could retrieve them. Pastor Turner took a different route back to the motel to avoid the police station.

Arrangements were already being made at the Mount Moriah Cemetery in Kansas City for the kids to be buried near George's dad. For the benefit of all the friends and neighbors in the lake area who knew the children, we decided to hold a memorial service at the Lakeland Baptist Church. It was scheduled for

2:00 the next day, Sunday, and Pastor Don Turner would officiate.

The hospital had been ordered not to tell Stephanie about the murders until George and I could be with her. However, the nurses neglected to remove the television from her room, and Steph learned about the deaths of her brothers and sisters on the Saturday morning news! The nurses tried to comfort her, but to no avail. We arranged to have her transported by an ambulance to Kansas City to be with relatives. Our plan was to drive to Kansas City immediately following the memorial service. We would join her there.

# THREE

# WHERE ARE MY KIDS NOW?

Time passed slowly in the motel room as we waited for news by phone or TV. It was now the second day after the children's deaths. By late morning we were all climbing the walls. We had never been in a room together without the patter of little feet around us. It was still several hours before another newspaper would hit the stands, so we waited. Finally I asked if we could go to the clinic to refill my birth-control pills. We all agreed that it would be good to get out of the room for a while.

I carried one of the newspapers with me, rolled into a cylinder, so I could keep the pictures and testimonies about my children close to me. It seemed this was the closest anybody was ever going to let me get to them.

As I rode in the back seat I gazed out at scenery I'd passed dozens of times, taking Steph to work and the boys to baseball practice. I don't think I had ever driven all the way to town without at least one of the kids with me. Never again would they pass this way with me. Excruciating loneliness gripped me.

I carried the rolled-up newspaper into the clinic with me. My mother accompanied me, leaving the men in the car. After giving my prescription to the pharmacist I joined Mom in the waiting area. Across the room, at the main desk, stood a young mother with a beautiful baby girl about 14 months old. I watched her intently as the mother passed the baby to a nurse so her hands would be free to write a check.

"Mom, I want to hold that baby," I said, trembling.

"No, honey, don't. It would only upset the mother."

Silently I watched as the nurse hugged and laughed with the baby. I listened to the mother talk happily to the nurse as if they were old friends. I missed Stacy so much. I wanted to touch her, to hug her, to take care of all her little needs.

"I've got to hold that baby," I pleaded.

"No!" Mom whispered firmly as she reached out to grab my hand.

I tried to make the feeling go away, but I desperately needed to touch that baby. I was tired of nobody letting me do what I must do. Unable to stand it any longer, and before Mom could stop me, I jumped up and hurried toward the mother.

She was still joking with the nurse when I broke in and, almost crying, asked, "Please, ma'am, may I hold your baby? I promise I won't hurt her. Just for a minute?"

The mother seemed puzzled at my tears. Her eyes questioningly met Mom's.

"This is the mother of the Swift children who were killed Thursday . . ."

Before Mom could finish the sentence the woman's eyes filled with tears. Quickly she reached over, took the baby from the nurse, and placed her in my arms. I set the newspaper on the desk to receive the child. It unrolled to reveal the pictures of my kids.

With the baby securely in my arms, the mother wrapped her arm around me and led me to a chair.

"You can hold her as long as you like," she cried.

Holding the infant girl on my lap, I gently caressed her fine blond hair and soft, tender skin. I admired her eyes and pixie features. She was so like Stacy!

All the commotion around her confused the child, and after only a few minutes she turned with out-stretched arms to her mother, who was now crying more than I was.

"I know. Mommies are special," I said to the child. "You can go back to your mommy if you want."

The mother took her baby and held her tight. After thanking her quietly for her understanding, I walked over to get my prescription. This woman will never know how very, very much her kindness helped me. I will never forget that baby's eyes looking into mine.

When we stepped back into the car I noticed Mom was crying. But I was not. I had done what I needed to do. My heart was satisfied for a little while.

As the sun sank lower in the sky that Saturday night, memories of the children overwhelmed me. The second day since their deaths on Thursday night was nearly gone, and I knew nothing more about how it had all happened. Even more intense was my need to know where they were now. I could not accept that they were actually lying in the morgue. Up till now I had felt that even though they were dead, they were still in the house. Now they'd been dead for two days. Were they in heaven? Or was there someplace else? When would I be with them again? Would I *ever* be with them again? As my thoughts intensified, my inner self throbbed and ached for the truth.

George and Dad went into town to get an evening newspaper. I told Mom that I was going into my room to sort out my feelings alone. Worried about me, she begged me to stay with her, but I insisted that I needed to be alone. She pleaded with me each step I took toward the door. Finally I could take no more.

"Please, Mom!" I half screamed. "I need to talk to God."

Complete silence filled the room as she looked stunned. More rational now, I turned to her. "Mom, I really do need to talk to God." Quietly I retreated into my own room.

The darkness enveloped me as I crossed to the farthest corner. There I sat on the floor facing the wall and closed my eyes. I felt like an empty 55-gallon drum, cold and empty.

The real me was a tiny speck inside the drum. It was screaming for answers, but its words only echoed back in the cold, empty space. The outside world was completely shut out. It couldn't—or wouldn't—give me the answers that I so desperately needed. I knew God couldn't be responsible for killing my kids. If this God that everybody talked about was so loving and merciful, He couldn't possibly have instigated all this. But was He really more sorry for the killers—as some had suggested—than He was for my kids?

"G-O-D!" the tiny speck screamed in desperation. "Please, God, H-E-A-R M-E!"

The tiny speck was quiet for a moment, hoping to

detect a response to its pleas.

"Please, God. I can't live without my kids. They're my whole life. What am I going to do with myself? I just can't survive without them. Don't You see? I can't do it. I'm not strong enough, God! I need them so badly. I'm nothing without them. I'm trying as hard as I can, but I'm just not strong enough. *Please,* bring them back. *Please!* I need them back! PLEASE, GOD, PLEASE!"

The voice echoed inside the steel drum. The noise was deafening. And then something happened. The echo faded away. Something punched a hole in the side of the drum, and a fluid, warm and comforting, began to fill it. The tiny speck basked in the security of the fluid, like a fetus in its womb. The drum filled, and as it did, my focus began to change. I realized that the drum was me, and the tiny speck was gone. The room came into focus and became the drum, except it didn't feel like a drum anymore, but rather like a warm, secure womb. For a long time I sat relishing this peaceful calmness. And then an answer, an assurance, came to me.

"You don't have to lose them," a voice seemed to say. "They are in My hands, and I am with you. I will give you My strength. I will help you to be strong enough."

All of a sudden it felt as if all my children were sitting on my lap. My arms caressed the air around me as I imagined touching and holding them. A tiny finger "reached up" to wipe away my tears.

Slowly and peacefully the feeling of the children on my lap began to fade away. When I realized that they were gone I turned to search for the voice again.

I listened intently to the words it spoke.

"You will be with them again. You have not lost them. You are separated from them for only a little while. It has all been taken care of. The answers you seek I will show you in My Book. I have written it all down for you."

The voice drifted away. I sat in the dark silence, waiting for more. None came. Still I stayed, reflecting on the things I'd heard and felt inside. There was no doubt that it all had been very real. I had not imagined any of it. I knew, as I rose from that corner, that God went with me. He would give me strength. I didn't have to fight this battle alone. Quietly I walked across the room, took a Bible from the desk drawer, and carefully opened its pages.

# FOUR

# THE FUNERAL

The memorial service at the Lakeland Baptist Church was scheduled for 2:00 Sunday afternoon. Friends and neighbors filled the sanctuary. My eyes met a particularly close friend whose children had played with our boys, and I could contain myself no more. I broke down and cried all the way up the aisle. Dad had told me to pull my shoulders back and walk proud. People would be watching me. But I just couldn't.

The service was comforting. Don Turner preached a short message summarizing the tragedy of four lost lives and the sacrifice that Christ had made for them. His words conveyed the love and concern that he felt for us. Afterward a man with a deep voice sang "Safe in the Arms of Jesus," which touched us so deeply that George asked Don for a copy of the song. Don found an old hymnal and tore the page out of it to give to him.

A room downstairs had been set up to allow friends to visit with us before we left town. Mrs. Larson, our next-door neighbor, was there, and she confirmed that the authorities had arrested Billy Dyer.

Debbie Balentine was there too. George hugged her tenderly, and we all cried together. She told us that she'd gotten a phone call from Stephanie Thursday night just before 8:00, asking if she'd mind going to our house to deliver a message from Stephanie. Debbie had entered the house to find Tonya, Stacy, and Steve dead. She did not see Greg, and in shock she began to call his name. When he didn't answer, she fled to call the police.

I wanted so badly to take all the terrible memories away from her. I knew that what she had seen still tormented her. She told me that when she saw Stacy on the floor the child's face and chest were all covered with blood, but her leg had only a trickle of blood on it. To mask the horror, her mind tried to tell her that Stacy was all right, that her leg was just scratched.

As we were saying our last goodbyes at the church, Steven and Mary came roaring up in their Blazer. He stuffed a wad of money into George's hand, money they had collected in a jar in just three days. Jars and memorial funds were set up all over town to help meet the enormous funeral expenses as well as Stephanie's medical bills. Every bank in the area was accepting funds, and local organizations were planning fund-raising events to collect even more. The whole world really was mourning the deaths of our children!

Customers were waiting at their restaurant and the waitress was trying to hold them at bay alone, so with teary hugs we said our goodbyes. Steven promised that they'd make it to Kansas City for the funeral and would keep in touch with Don Turner as to the day and time. They jumped back into their vehicle and sped away.

We left for Kansas City. As I quietly watched the beautiful scenery of the Ozarks flash by my back seat window, I realized that I was departing my home for good. I was leaving behind all my friends, all the people who banded together and took the time to care. Everything that connected my life with my kids was getting farther and farther away. Soon city streets would replace the scenery of the Ozarks. For a brief moment I panicked. It made no sense to return to the big, noisy city. I was a part of those hills. They were a part of me and my children. Something made me look up into the sky just then, and there, flying with us directly overhead, were four mallard ducks.

"Oh, George," I cried, "look at the ducks!"

For as long as I could remember we'd watched for the ducks this time of year as they migrated south for the winter. George and I stared at them in silence, entranced with the grace and precision with which they flew. Tears began to blur my vision.

"Oh, George," I whimpered, "I wish the kids could see them."

He turned to me with just a glint of a smile. "Maybe they are the ones who sent them," he said softly.

I looked out again to see the ducks still overhead. Maybe the children had sent them. I gazed in awe and wonder. Maybe the voice that had spoken to me the previous night in the motel room had sent the ducks to comfort me. I watched them until they veered to the south and disappeared. We rode in silence the rest of the way, each of us engulfed in our our thoughts.

Stephanie was lying on the couch when we arrived at my parents' apartment. She looked so frail and white. My father knelt beside her and spoke quietly. "You know, Steph, you're my only granddaughter now, and I love you very much. I want to be with you at the funeral. Do you think you'll be strong enough to walk?"

Steph shook her head.

"You know that if my back were stronger I'd carry you all the way. I'm just afraid my old back won't take it. But I'll see if we can arrange a wheelchair for you if you think that would be easier for you."

The girl responded with a grateful hug.

"I love you, Steph, I really do," Dad cried.

Monday morning we gathered at the Mount Moriah Funeral Home and Cemetery to begin making arrangements for the service. The funeral home was located on the cemetery grounds. Expecting a large number of guests, we decided to hold the service at Mount Moriah rather than at a church in order to avoid a long drive to the cemetery.

The evening newspaper announced that Ray Richardson had been arraigned at 2:00 p.m., charged with four counts of capital murder and ordered held without bond pending trial. Deputy Sheriff Skipper Hedges told reporters that they had a motive for the killings, but he refused to divulge it, saying, "Once you knew what it [the motive] is—if you ever know, if it eventually comes out in court—you'll know why we can't say anything. Certain aspects of the case may never be revealed."

We were puzzled and never have found out what he meant.

When we arrived at the funeral home Tuesday morning the kids had been dressed, placed in their caskets, and taken to the chapel ready for the service the following day. The caskets sat side by side, Tonya and Stacy in the middle flanked by Greg and Steve. It seemed only natural to have the boys protecting their baby sisters.

Touching each casket, we spoke softly and lovingly to the child that lay inside. I wanted so badly to open the lids and touch my babies once more. But I had made a promise to Dad. He did not want me to see their injuries.

Several times during the last few days we had talked about opening the caskets. I didn't want to see them just to find out what was wrong with them. I needed to see them one last time. I found myself caught between my promise to Dad and my intense need to touch my kids one more time. That evening I asked the funeral director if he thought it would be wise to see the kids.

"They really don't look bad," he said. "You do what's in your heart. Don't let anybody tell you what to do, because tomorrow they'll be buried and it will be too late."

That was all I needed.

"I do want to see them," I said. "But first we have to go buy bonnets for the girls. Dad said if I insisted on seeing them they must have bonnets."

"We can push their heads deeper in the pillows," the director offered.

"No, I want to get bonnets. We'll be right back."

Although we went to three stores, none of them had any bonnets. It was close to 9:00 when we returned to Mount Moriah to tell the funeral directors that we'd be back in the morning. We drove quietly back to my parents' house.

Early Wednesday morning we went out to find bonnets for the girls. To our surprise, the first store we went to had a whole tableful of them on sale at a dollar apiece! We bought two and drove directly to the funeral home.

The funeral home opened the caskets and put the bonnets on before we were once again escorted into the chapel.

I'll never regret my decision to see the kids. No open wounds were visible. Greg, who had died from a single bullet, actually looked peaceful. Stacy's cheeks were puffed and purple, and Steve's jaw appeared to be open, though his lips were closed. Tonya's eyes were closed tight in a squint, as if she had tried to block out the things happening to her.

I stood there looking down on the still forms of my children. What had they been through those last horrible moments? Did they cry for help? Did they know that no one would hear? Could I have stopped it had I been home?

As I looked more closely at Steve he seemed to breathe. I laid my hand on his chest. He was so cold. His chest was like a solid block. It didn't move. My blurring eyes studied his 14-year-old form.

"You became a man that night, Steve," I whispered. "You didn't let us down. I know you watched the girls like I told you to, and I know you'll take good care of them in heaven till I can be there too. I love you, Steve, and I miss you so badly."

Seeing the kids had taken a great weight off me. I could now begin to accept their deaths. Finally I could say goodbye—but only for a little while. "I'd like to get four long-stemmed roses that I could give the kids to be buried with them," I told the funeral director. "It's kind of a tradition with George and me to show our love for each other that way. May I do that?"

"Of course you can," he said. An hour later I had the roses, and we returned to the chapel to place one in each child's hand, telling them again how much we loved them and that the rose would be a sign between us of that love.

Dad came later to apologize for trying to talk me out of seeing the kids. "I'm sorry. I didn't realize— would it offend you?" Dad hesitated, looking from George to me. "I just gotta see them too."

"You have to do what's in your heart," George replied.

An hour later Dad returned, crying. "I'm sorry, George. Joy. I hope you don't get mad at me, but Tonya got to me one last time."

"What do you mean, Dad?" we asked.

"I had chewing gum in my front pocket," he wept. "She asked me for it. I couldn't resist her so—I put the whole pack of gum in her other hand next to the rose." He could barely finish without breaking up.

Never again would his Sunshine climb into his lap and say, "Pa, you got any gum?" We all hugged each other and cried. Dad regained his composure and went in to see the kids for a few minutes more before going home to bring Mom to the funeral.

We remained in the office while the guests arrived. The chapel overflowed, and they had to open the double doors to an adjoining room to hold the crowd.

We entered the family seating area to find it filled beyond capacity. Steven, Mary, and Don Turner had come, bringing a classmate of Steve's with them. Stephanie sat, thin and trembling, in a wheelchair in the front row with Jean beside her. The service began as soon as we were seated.

I remember little of the service, catching snatches of what Father Firth was saying. My mind kept drifting away to recall happy times our family had spent together.

My only regret, as I studied the faces in the crowd, was that none of these people would ever have a chance to know how truly special and unique my children had been or how extremely proud I had been to be their mother.

A limousine chauffeured us to the grave site where the caskets were set on stands above a single hole 16 feet long. The children were buried side by side in the order of their ages from Stacy to Steve, with an extra plot next to Steve already purchased for Stephanie. We all hoped that Steph would beat the cancer and would not need it for many years to come, but we knew that those chances were slim.

The graveside service was short, and people slowly began to filter away. I felt a tremendous desire to grab a shovel and start filling in the enormous hole. Although I stifled the desire, to this day I think it would have done me some good. The strenuous exercise might have helped release all the anger I held inside. As it was, those feelings stayed inside to eat away at me for months.

The funeral home arranged a large room afterward so we could visit with friends. We hadn't held a regular visiting hour the night before, so we stayed several hours talking to people, comforting them and being comforted.

Little by little the crowd thinned out. The funeral was over. We had spent the past several days making the last preparations we would ever be able to for our children. But now there was nothing left to do for them. No more plans to discuss about their futures. So many dreams were buried with them that day. The realization that we would never be able to touch them again was just beginning to sink in.

# DR. HORSEMAN

The day after the funeral service an ambulance took Stephanie back to the hospital in Columbia. We had considered transferring her to a Kansas City hospital, but we felt that the doctors had already started a good program for Steph at the hospital in Columbia, and she had become very close to the nurses there. Right now she needed all the familiar faces she could get.

I too needed familiar faces. My feelings of uselessness bore deep inside of me as I came to grips with the fact that my responsibilities to my four children were forever over on this earth. I longed to hold them, to touch them once more. But I could not.

I had never left my children with anyone I did not know or trust. For the first time I was not certain where they were. *Are they really in heaven with a loving Father?* I wondered. *What is God really like? Can I trust Him to take care of all their little needs? Will He give them the same love and attention that I did?* I wanted to be with them. "They need me!" my heart cried out. "I want to leave this earth more than anything in the world. Why can't I go? Why can't I be with my babies?" I felt so worthless without them.

Suddenly I realized that I was very near the brink of self-destruction. With no desire to eat, I had lost weight. My cheekbones stuck out more than ever before. My insides ached constantly. I knew that I needed help—someone I could trust. Picking up the phone, I called Dr. Robert Horseman.

I had been only 15, unmarried and pregnant, when I met him for the first time. Never talking down to me or trying to judge me, he just called me Little One. In the delivery room he sang humorous little operatic ditties to ease my labor. More than my doctor, he was my friend.

I arrived at Dr. Horseman's office at 4:30 that afternoon. All his other patients had gone home. Only his nurses remained. One of them took me into an examining room, weighed me, and took my blood pressure.

Dr. Horseman entered and his eyes met mine. The tears burst from inside me as all the pain and anguish rushed out at once. Dr. Horseman sat down, and without a word took me by the hand and sat me on his lap. Then holding me in his arms as he would a child, he rocked me slowly back and forth. I cried there on his shoulder for a very long time, expressing in words only half the feelings that I held inside.

"You do understand, don't you?" my heart silently pled. "You knew how precious my children were from the moment they were born. You do understand how much a part of my life they were."

Though few words were spoken, I knew that he did understand.

The nurse prepared a tray of instruments. Dr. Horseman left the room while the nurse assisted me into a gown. He returned a few minutes later to give me a complete checkup. Then I dressed and met him in his office.

He advised me to cut down on cigarettes and to work up to eating regularly. "And if you ever need someone to talk to," he said, "remember that I'll be here anytime." As I left his office my burden was easier to bear.

We learned through the newspaper that Billy Dyer had been charged with delinquency in the killings. He was to undergo psychological tests at the Missouri Department of Mental Health in Columbia before the juvenile court heard his case. We didn't like the idea of Billy being so close to the hospital where Steph was. In fact, we didn't want to be anywhere near him. But there wasn't anything we could do about it.

We spent most of the next two weeks with Stephanie, renting a room at a motel a few miles away so we could be with her all day. I spent many hours sitting in the hall outside her hospital room reading the Bible, trying to learn more about the God who was now responsible for my children's welfare. My sister had given us a paraphrased paperback called *The Way* for our first Christmas. Dad brought it from the house when he got our clothes. Keeping it with me, I read it every chance I had.

I made the mistake of starting on page one and found the wars and killings of the Old Testament appalling. Thus I got almost no comfort out of it, and very few answers to my many questions. When I asked for a minister to come to the chapel at the hospital to talk to me, even he was not able to answer my questions. He did not know the biblical answers for why I was going through all this pain and loss. Why didn't he point out Job to me? Job was a man who suffered greatly under Satan's hand, including losing all his children, and yet he lived to rise above it all. I felt like Job. But at the time I had never heard of him. My sister pointed him out to me many months later.

Right now I was even more confused. Why couldn't a minister provide me with answers? Ever since that afternoon in the corner of the motel room I knew with great conviction that my answers were in the Bible. But I would have to seek them out myself. I continued to read the Bible, and I asked questions of anyone who would listen.

September 27, five days after the funeral, we returned to Mount Moriah. It was Tonya's fourth birthday. We bought a bouquet of yellow daisies with lots of baby's breath. I attached a handwritten card sealed in plastic, and we drove to the grave site. There I carefully placed the flowers at the head of Tonya's grave and reread the card I'd put so much thought into.

"Dear Tonya,

"Today is your fourth birthday. I had such plans. I wanted to build you a toy stove and refrigerator so you could cook like me. And a stuffed deer like the real ones we'd seen on the road. And a yellow bicycle with training wheels. And a big chocolate cake. But it seems that all I can give you now is pretty flowers and the knowledge that Daddy and I are fine and thinking of you always. We can be robbed of our lives, but no one can steal our souls. We'll all meet again someday in God's great paradise. I love you, honey, so very much.

"You keep an eye on Stacy and help Greg and Steve until Daddy and I can join you. Someday soon, baby, someday soon . . .

"Love, Mommy"

Still not completely sure that the kids were being cared for properly in heaven, I was depending more on their being responsible for each other. I was thankful that Steve was old enough to handle the job. He had so many things yet to teach Stacy. So many responsibilities toward his brother and sisters. Responsibilities that used to be mine. I ached to go and help him so that he could run and play without care. It wasn't fair to place so much on a 14-year-old boy. But I knew that I could trust him to be responsible.

We left the cemetery many tears later and returned to Columbia to be with our last surviving child.

CHAPTER
## SIX

# GOODBYE, STEPHANIE

The mental anguish of burying her brothers and sisters, added to the physical pain caused by the cancer, was more than Steph's body could fight at once.

"Dad, I'm the only one left," she cried as he held her in his arms. The loss of the other four had greatly weakened her desire to live and fight the disease. Each day Stephanie slipped further away from us. Fluid collected in her abdomen and swelled her body horribly. The tumor that lay against her spine caused her enormous agony. A tube ran from her side to the fluid-collection bag and another tube to a catheter, making it impossible for her to roll over on her stomach. She adjusted the head and foot of her electric bed continually, trying to find a comfortable position to lie in. Small noises greatly upset her.

We tried to get her to brush her own hair and do a few things for herself, but her muscles wouldn't work for her. She was like an invalid. George and I found it difficult to sit with her for very long, seeing her so wasted, so we took turns. Eating all our meals at the hospital cafeteria, we rarely left the hospital before nightfall.

Every waking moment was agonizingly painful for her. She begged hourly for a stronger injection to kill the pain, but the dosage was never completely effective. Mercifully, she slept much of the time, her eyelids half opened.

One morning a nurse came to weigh her. By now Stephanie was so weak that she could not stand alone. Fluid bloated her abdomen, while her arms and legs were skin and bones. The nurse and I worked together to raise her and ease her legs over the edge of the bed. Steph cried to be put back down. We managed to get her off the bed and onto the scales. While I held her on one side and the nurse the other, Stephanie still couldn't support enough of her own weight for us to get an accurate reading. The scales tipped back and forth under her feet, terrifying her. She begged to lie down again.

Holding her tightly, mustering all the strength and courage I had within me, I turned to look at George, who was watching from the door. Pain filled his face. His only remaining child was dying, and there was nothing he could do for her. He fled from the room before the tears burst.

After that, Steph was only semiconscious most of the time. Her body was exhausted from trying to fight the disease. The nurses fed her only liquids, because she no longer had the strength to chew. She had no desire to watch TV or listen to the radio. Her eyes were so strained that she had given up reading weeks before. Hooked up to a heart monitoring machine, she had someone with her constantly. All day long she just lay there.

At times I thought she was completely unaware that I was there with her. But when I stood to tiptoe out of the room, she would suddenly ask, "Where are you going?" and I would sit back down to endure the dark silence a little longer, the steady blip of the monitor assuring me that she was still alive.

Stephanie was actually alert one afternoon, and we were so happy to see her awake and talking that George and I stayed with her together. Steph pushed the nurse call button beside her bed to request some ice water. For days she'd been too weak to ask for anything. Two nurses came sprinting down the hall and burst into her room. Their looks of panic frightened Steph. They thought it was an emergency and that we had pushed the button in alarm. The nurses began to laugh foolishly to ease Stephanie's mind, but it didn't work.

Steph never knew she had cancer. The only word used around her was tumor. For the first time, I think Steph realized she was going to die. "Dad," she asked softly, "do they have an American Tumor Society?"

An enormous lump rose in George's throat. He just didn't know how to answer her.

On October 4 Steph was in a terrible amount of pain and begged to skip her chemotherapy treatment. We watched as the nurses fought to get her on a gurney to wheel her downstairs. She clung tightly to a stuffed toy dog as if it were her only friend, and pleaded loudly to be allowed to stay in her room. George and I followed as they wheeled her out into the hall.

Stephanie no longer looked like a young woman of 17, confident about her future. Now she reminded me of an innocent 5-year-old being carried away against her will. I thought about all the things the police and others had refused to let me do after the kids had been killed, and my mind couldn't handle watching the same thing happen to my last child. George's heart broke, too, and he told them to take her back to her room.

Escaping to the elevator before Stephanie could see the pain written across my face, I went straight to the chapel downstairs. There I walked boldly up to the altar and knelt down to pray. I wanted to be face-to-face with God.

"Please, God," I prayed, "don't let her hurt any more. She's been through enough. Make her better, and if You can't make her better now, then please, have mercy and take her instead. She can't bear any more. Please, God, take her now!"

I stood then, my hands clenched firmly against my sides, grinding my teeth in outrage. My entire body shook with anger at the injustice my family was being dealt. Why must my children suffer so? There must be an end to it all.

Suddenly the tears of anger burst forth, and my body sobbed in great heaves. I fell into the front pew and buried my face in my hands. I cried there a long time before I could gain enough composure to return to the waiting room upstairs. Steph slipped into unconsciousness once more, and we went back to the motel for the evening.

At 9:00 George felt he urgently needed to go see Stephanie. He sensed something was wrong, though he told me to stay and rest. I was in bed when he returned an hour and a half later. He woke me with a kiss.

"Everything's going to be OK," he said softly. "Before I left I said, 'Steph, I love you.' She opened her eyes and said, 'I love you too, Dad.'" He paused. "I just know everything's going to be OK. I was really worried when I left, but now I'm OK. She's going to be all right."

My husband went to bed at peace with himself.

George had already showered when I woke up the next morning and was dressing to go to the hospital. When I started to get up to join him, he told me to sleep a while longer. It was only 7:30. Knowing that I was exhausted, he said he'd come back around 9:30 to get me. But at 9:00 someone knocked at my door. I opened it to find the motel clerk standing outside.

"I got a call from your husband," she said. "He wants you to take a cab to the hospital right away."

"What's the matter?" I asked. "Did he say what was wrong?"

"No, he just said to come quickly. If you like, I'll go down and call you a taxi."

When I arrived at the hospital I rushed for the elevator. It seemed far slower than it had the 100 odd other times I'd ridden it the past weeks. As the elevator doors opened on the third floor, George stepped into it. He looked at me, relieved that I was there.

"It's all over, honey," he said quietly. "She's gone."

"No!" I cried. "I didn't get to say goodbye!"

His voiced quavered. "None of us did, honey," he whispered.

Suddenly my head was dizzy. My legs no longer

wanted to hold me up. It felt as if another part of my heart had just been ripped away. I had wanted to be with her that last moment, to help her, comfort her. Why had I slept this morning? Now it was too late. I ached so badly inside, an ache that I was beginning to get used to, and yet each time it hurt even more. She'd been dead only a few minutes, and already I missed her terribly.

The long drive from Columbia back to Kansas City was quiet and lonely. George and I talked little. We tried to lose our thoughts in the trees and hills that passed by. Neither of us felt the turmoil that we'd experienced with the deaths of the other four. They had been brutally and senselessly murdered. With Steph, it was different. Her death brought an end to her pain and suffering and seemed only merciful in comparison.

Early that afternoon we arrived back at my parents' house and told Dad about Steph. A stack of mail had been waiting for us for more than a week. The first one I opened was from Dr. Horseman. "We regret to inform you that your pap smear has come back positive for cancer cells. Please call the office. . . ."

Angrily I threw the letter down.

"No!" I yelled. "It can't be! The very day my last child dies of cancer they tell me I've got it too! I can't do it. I was strong for Stephanie, but I'm not strong enough to go through it myself." I thought of all the horrible tests Steph had undergone, the excruciating pain she had lived with, her begging to be relieved. And I thought of the prayer I'd asked just the night before for God to either heal her or let her die. Although I felt guilty for my request, at the same time

I felt thankful to Him for ending her suffering.

"Goodbye, George," I said sarcastically. "I'm as good as gone too. I might as well jump out a window and end it quickly. It sure would save me a lot of pain. You're the last of the Swifts, now."

I ranted and raved as George quietly sat on the couch, eyes blurring, unable to say anything and scared to death that it was all going to come true.

"Please, Joy," Dad pleaded. "Go call the doctor and talk to him."

Furious, I paced the floor back and forth, back and forth. Finally I stopped at the phone and dialed. When Dr. Horseman came to the line I didn't even say hello.

"What is this, the final kick in the teeth?"

He didn't understand.

"My last child just died of cancer this morning, and I get back into town, and the first thing I read says I've got cancer!"

"Calm down now," the doctor soothed. "The tests showed a very faint positive. It may be nothing at all. I'd like to put you in the hospital for a couple days, do a biopsy and conization, and if it's cancer, chances are it's so minute we can take care of it then. It's not worth getting this upset about."

"OK," I answered, calmed a bit but still sarcastic. "When do you want me? I'll be there in an hour if you say so."

My husband hollered from the other room. "No, honey. If it can wait, let's get through the funeral first."

The funeral! In my fit I'd forgotten about it. That would be Friday. We arranged for me to enter the

Shawnee Mission Medical Center the following Tuesday.

Mount Moriah was beginning to feel like a second home as we returned to make even more funeral arrangements. The service was held the afternoon of October 7, which happened to be my dad's birthday.

Throughout the service I kept my eye on the casket, covered with a purple drape and a spray of roses. I thought about all the wonderful times and happy smiles we'd had with Steph. Then I recalled the painful, agonizing weeks Steph had spent in the hospital and felt relieved that for her it was over. She looked normal again, at peace, unswollen in that casket. Now she was in heaven with all her brothers and sisters. How could I be sad? My tears were selfish, for I missed them all terribly and longed to be with them. But my kids were in a better place, and I was left here to endure grief and loneliness until that time when I could join them.

Communion was offered, and I was the first one up to receive it. For the first time in my life I began to feel the service's meaning: that Jesus Christ had died not just for me, but, more important, for my children, in order that they might live again in a world without pain or suffering. I now felt that I must prove myself worthy of obtaining this paradise that Jesus had promised. I wanted Him to be proud of me, proud of the way I was enduring this horrible loss, proud of how I was reading the Bible to learn the truth about death, life everlasting, and the tremendous love He felt for me. I must prove myself worthy of such love. Realizing that Jesus, too, had suffered and endured, I felt a great strength and warmth. He was my example to follow, to try patiently to endure and live out my life, learning about God and making myself needed. I had a whole life ahead of me while I waited to see my kids again.

It was at this point that I realized I must start a new family, not to replace the ones I had lost, but to give my life meaning, to make myself useful, to feel important and have a definite place on earth while I was still here. Perhaps the years would pass more quickly if I was busy, until someday I could be with my kids again. Finally I felt at peace.

At the end of the service they ushered us out while they prepared the casket for transport to the burial site. The young man from the funeral home walked up to me carrying a single, long-stemmed rose. He remembered how important it had been for me to give the other kids a rose. I'll never forget his kindness.

The funeral staff allowed me a few minutes alone with Steph to place the rose in her hand and say goodbye. Praise God, she looked so peaceful. I told her about the hope that I would be with them all someday soon, that I'd do my best to make them proud of me. After all, they now had the wisdom of angels, and I had much to learn about God's Word and His truth. Little did I know how very much I had to learn.

A hole had been dug right next to Steve's grave. Steph's burial was not as traumatic as burying the other kids. I felt no urgent desire to wield a shovel and plow into the earth. We lingered after all the others had gone home. Then my whole family returned to my parents' house to be with Dad on what was left of his birthday.

# MY ORDEAL

With the funeral behind us George contemplated the next hurdle in our paths. In four days I was scheduled to go to the hospital. The thought of what the doctors might find scared him to death. If he lost me too, he vowed, he would run for the mountains and live like a hermit the rest of his life. Everything was happening too fast. He was in shock, numb and afraid, and yet he was so busy trying to comfort others, trying to convince them that he would be fine, that many months later he told a priest that he'd never even had a chance to cry it all out himself.

Tuesday morning I packed slowly, not eager to get to the Shawnee Mission Medical Center. George and I said little to each other along the way. I tried to be calm as we entered the hospital. Although I always prided myself for being a model patient, the memory of the tests Steph had gone through kept unsettling my thoughts. George stayed in a waiting area with my bag while someone escorted me into a cubicle beside the lab. As I watched the nurse prepare an oversized hypodermic needle with which to draw some blood, I began to panic. The needle entered my arm and blood filled the clear tube, making me shudder violently.

"This is ridiculous," I said, trying to reason with myself. "It's only a blood test." But with each test that followed I became more panic-stricken and aware that I, like Stephanie, might not leave this place alive.

I received a room on the second floor. George stayed quietly with me all day, unable to find any words to comfort me. During the past weeks with Steph he had tried not to give up, but no matter how hard he tried, he had stood helpless, unable to save his daughter. No amount of love that he might hold for her could save her. Death had shown no mercy to the constant ache and emptiness he carried. Now he had only one person left to love, and he felt utterly helpless. Whatever happened during the next few days was completely out of his hands, and the anguish of not knowing our future was overwhelming.

The nurses shooed him out just after 8:00 p.m., and he returned to my parents' house. Early the next morning he arrived to be with me before the operation. Dr. Horseman came in to give us a few details. Cervical cancer usually begins at the opening of the cervix, he told us. He would remove a tiny cone-shaped section out of that area for examination. The lab would cut this section into ultra thin slices to be put under a microscope. If cancer cells were found, they would proceed from there.

Later that afternoon Dr. Horseman notified us that the lab results were complete.

"The tests showed that there definitely were cancer cells present," he began.

Fear gripped my entire body.

"But," he continued, "they were all contained within the opening of the cervix, and when we cut out that little cone, it appears that we got them all."

An almost painful sigh of relief came simultaneously from George and me as our hands gripped tightly together.

*I'm actually going to get to walk out of this place,* my mind screamed in triumph.

He warned me, however, never to take birth control pills again and to get a pap smear every six months to ensure that the cancer did not return. My heart sank all over again as my eyes met his. Was I going to have to fight this all my life?

"Don't worry," he said. "If we catch it early, we can do the same thing we did today. That's why we've got to have those pap smears—to catch it in its first stages. It may never come back at all."

"OK," I said, feeling a little less victorious than I had before.

"By the way," he commented as he prepared to leave, "I want you to wait at least three months before you try to get pregnant again. Let's let that cervix heal first."

"Yes, sir!" I saluted as he walked out the door.

I was OK! I had a future to start thinking about. In three months we could start a new family. Could I wait that long?

After George left the hospital that evening a faint sound from the other end of the hall caught my ear—newborns crying in the nursery. I longed to hold one of them. Mine were all dead, and I couldn't touch them anymore.

Pulling the family picture from the bedside stand, I sat up in bed to admire the beautiful faces of my children. I held the picture close to my face, speaking softly to them, needing them so badly. Tears filled my eyes and rolled down my cheeks until I couldn't see anymore. My insides ached, unable to fulfill this desperate need to touch my children. Would my heart ever be as full as it once was? Would I ever be truly happy again? How could I be without my children? They had filled my life so fully. It seemed so empty now. I had so many years still ahead of me. How could I learn to live with this loneliness? I felt that even if I did have another baby, it could never fill the enormous void that the other kids had left. If I had 10 more children, it would never be filled.

*Why does this room have to be so quiet?* I thought. *I'd give anything to hear a familiar laugh. Just a chuckle. One more "Hey, what's for dinner?" "Has anybody seen my baseball?" "Mommy, I need a drink."*

"God, please bring them back," I pleaded. "I can't live with this emptiness forever."

A nurse walked by my door and heard me crying. She came in and sat beside me. "Are you OK?" she asked.

"I don't know. I miss my kids so badly," I cried, as the tears spilled out once more. "I heard all the newborns going in to see their mothers, and I can't ever touch my babies again."

"You'll get to touch them again someday," she said.

"But I need to touch them now. I know they're in God's hands. I talked with Him the day after they were killed, and He told me that they were with Him. I don't know much about God, though. I've been reading the Bible to find out, but I'm not sure about when I may get to be with them again. How can I be sure that I'm even worthy of being with them again? It's the most important thing in my life!"

"Well, I'm a Seventh-day Adventist," she said, "and we believe that Jesus is coming again very soon. When He does, you will see your children again."

"But when?" I asked. "In my lifetime?"

"The Bible says that only God knows the day, but that we should be ready. The time is very near. Keep looking in the Bible and pray that the Holy Spirit will guide you. The Bible says, 'Seek and ye shall find' [Matthew 7:7]. You will find your answers."

She took the picture from my hand. "They're beautiful children. You must have been very proud of them."

"They were the best," I replied.

She laid the picture beside me and took the Bible from the stand by my bed. Then turning its pages, she handed the Bible to me. I read the passage she pointed out:

"For the Lord himself shall descend from heaven with a shout, with the voice of the archangel, and with the trump of God: and the dead in Christ shall rise first. Then we which are alive and remain shall be caught up together with them in the clouds, to meet the Lord in the air; and so shall we ever be with the Lord. Wherefore comfort one another with these words" (1 Thessalonians 4:16-18).

They were the most wonderful words I had ever read.

"You just keep looking here," she said, pointing to

the open Bible. "And if you need anyone to talk to or if you have any questions, you just call on me. I'm a good listener, and I've got a broad shoulder to cry on."

"Thank you," I said as she rose to leave.

I was filled with a new hope and a great desire to find out more about when Jesus would return so I could be with my kids again. The babies down the hall didn't matter anymore. I had five children already, and I was going to be with them again. I thought of the glorious day when Jesus will appear in the sky and take me to be with my kids. I imagined the shrill sound of the trumpet announcing to people all over the world that the time has come, and the faces of all the grieving mothers and fathers looking toward heaven as Jesus Christ descends in the sky. What a fantastic sight that will be!

I read through the night, thumbing through various sections of the Old and New Testaments. The Bible had everything: how to raise your kids, how to be a good wife, how to treat others, morals, standards of living, prophecies, and most of all love, hope, and wisdom. *This is a terrific book,* I thought. *Why was I so lost when the answers have been within my grasp all along?* I could not absorb it all fast enough. My thirst for knowledge was unquenchable. I *would* seek, and I *would* find. I would make my kids proud.

Two days later I left the hospital and returned to my parents' house. Mom and I spent our evenings looking at her photo albums and matching up the negatives to any pictures that had the kids in them. She gave me all the photos, explaining that she would get reprints for herself. Many were not dated, so I decided to try to date them. Some were easy, such as those of birthdays and holidays. Others were more difficult. I had to study each one to match up haircuts, seasonal clothing, and other details to date them by month and year.

Mom cried a lot while we went through the photos, but I did not. I had a fresh, new hope and wanted to relish the moments depicted in these photos and memorize the looks on the children's faces. I ran back and forth between the dining room and the living room to share a special pose of Tonya with Pa or a happy time with George. We had had so many wonderful times with the kids. I didn't ever want to forget a single day of our lives together. Nothing could ever erase my memories of them. Each of them had made a definite impression on this earth while they were alive. They had touched so many people. So many days had been happy just because they were there. My memory was the most important thing I owned right then. It would have to carry me through all the years until Jesus returned to take me to be with them. Then we would have even more happy times when Jesus came back. I looked with all my heart for that wonderful reunion day and prayed that it would be very soon.

# EIGHT

# LIFE BEGINS OVER AGAIN

George was getting restless at my parents' house and wanted to escape to western Kansas, but we felt that we would somehow be letting people down by going. We thought about it for days, but talked ourselves out of it every time. One evening, visiting one of my husband's friends named Roy, we expressed our desire to get away for a while. Neither of us knew what we wanted to do about a house or a job yet.

The rest of the evening we continued to think about the question but didn't reach any decision. Roy came out to the car to see us off.

"Just go home, pack some clothes, and go," he said. "Don't ask anybody if it's OK. Just go. Get out of here for a while. You both need it. You need to be alone for a while."

On the way home we decided to leave in the morning.

The drive to St. Francis was truly peaceful. I enjoyed being alone with George, the man I'd loved all my life and the only person left in the world who really mattered to me. It's a long drive from Kansas City to St. Francis, and it felt odd to drive so far without a single "Dad, how many more miles?" or "I have to go potty." But somehow, with just the two of us alone, I could pretend that the kids were with us and we were still a family. Occasionally, when I saw a particularly pretty cloud, I would watch it for miles, thinking that perhaps the kids were sitting on the cloud peering over the edge and watching us as we went along. It made me feel close to them and strengthened my desire to learn more about God so they would be proud of me.

We spent several weeks with our friends Dee and Hookie. Hookie and his son Charlie were busy building a road between two fields, and George got to drive the road grader back and forth, moving dirt into the middle and creating drainage ditches on either side. Sometimes I rode with him in the big cab. It was tranquility itself going slowly back and forth, seeing nothing but wheat and sky. I looked around the cab and figured out a way to get all five of the kids in there with us. It would be tight, but we would all fit. I rode along, contentedly making up little things the kids would say if they were really here, and watching for little things that might have caught their eyes.

In the evenings Dee and I went though the stacks of photos that I'd brought along with me. I told her about each one and put them in order for dating. George did a little pheasant hunting, and we took lots of pictures with our new camera.

Probably we overstayed our welcome, though Dee and Hookie never indicated so. But I loved it so much out there. With all that land around us there was no need to worry about what the neighbors thought or what the people in town were doing. We could just go at our own pace. Everybody else was too far away to care. The pressure that had built up inside started to dissipate. I spent a lot of time sitting alone in a field watching the sky and losing myself in fantasy. Reality still hurt too much to live with it every moment. I lived for those moments when I could dream.

When we finally did return to Kansas City, we were ready to start facing everyday commitments again. George took a job working security at a construction company on strike. We rented a house across town on December 1 and made arrangements to retrieve our stored belongings from Camdenton.

It was no easy task emotionally going through all the kids' toys and clothes. During the evenings I tried to organize all their things into individual boxes to keep in a back room. George worked nights and came home around 3:00 a.m. It became a habit for me to stay up till he got home. I'd have a nice dinner waiting. Then we'd go to bed just before dawn and sleep far into the afternoon. It may have seemed strange to some, but George was all I had left to take care of, so I adjusted my schedule to his. We called each other often while he was working, especially when one of us reached an emotional crisis and needed comforting.

One night after midnight I was going through a box of Stephanie's things and dropped a piece of paper on the floor in front of the couch. I got down on hands and knees to find it, and there in the metal frame of the couch, directly below the place I'd been sitting, I saw a mark where a bullet had hit and ricocheted. I felt paralyzed. That bullet had been aimed at Steve, who had been sitting in this exact spot when I had left him that night. The first bullet had caused him to fall to the floor. He crawled under the couch in an attempt to save himself, but Billy returned to fire more shots at him. This bullet missed its mark, but four others had not. I called George to tell him what I had found.

Little by little I organized our things and found blood on many of them. Stacy's punch balloon was popped and badly spattered with blood. Tiny drops had sprinkled the mirror and drawers of my dresser. I knew it had to be Tonya's blood. She had been shot in my bed only three feet away. It's very hard to look at blood and realize that it belonged to your children. One part of you wants to reject it. Another part wants to cling to it as a tangible piece of someone you loved—their life-giving blood. But it was not giving them life anymore. It had been shed in death.

On December 13 we learned that the juvenile court had waived jurisdiction of Billy Dyer, which, in effect, made him an adult. The state charged him with four counts of capital murder. To us, this was a small victory. Instead of being charged with delinquency, there was now a chance that he might be punished for the crime he had committed.

When I finally had all the children's personal belongings organized into one room I brought George in to share it with me. It was my favorite place to be, surrounded by Greg's matchbox cars, the chess set Steve had made in shop class, Tonya's macaroni necklace, and Steph's favorite shawl. Many expressed concern that I stayed home alone with all these memories around me, suggesting that I get a job to keep me busy and make new friends. But I was used to being in charge of my own domain and my own time. For a time I considered taking some art courses, but never got around to it, the main reason being that I began feeling sick in the mornings. After two weeks of nausea I called Dr. Horseman. A visit to his office confirmed my suspicions. I was pregnant, and I hadn't waited three months.

I still spent much time reading the Bible, and each discovery brought more joy. A few months before, I had received a letter from a Mrs. Brents in Memphis, Tennessee. She wrote that the devil, not God, was to blame for our troubles. I never did blame God. A great Being such as He couldn't have wanted my children to die like that.

Mrs. Brents explained that God had not wanted people to die at all. He had warned Adam and Eve against sin, but the devil had caused them to disobey, and the wages of sin is death. She said that death was only a sleep until the resurrection, which was soon to come. We did not go at the moment of death to a heavenly paradise. God promised that we would be resurrected to life on earth.

This amazed me. All my life I had thought that when Christians died they went to heaven. The nurse at the hospital had talked about the resurrection too. But I was not clear on where my children were until Jesus came back. I knew only that I would be reunited with them. Mrs. Brents said that the kids were simply sleeping in their graves until Christ's coming. If that was true, I could handle that. They were at least feeling no pain. But I had never heard that we would be resurrected on earth. This new information excited me.

"I would be happy to discuss and share more Bible thoughts with you," Mrs. Brents offered in her letter.

Yes! I wanted to know it all. At last someone was offering some answers. I wrote back to her that I was starved for knowledge and wanted to know all about God's promise to raise my kids back to life.

I received her reply just before Christmas. "It makes our hearts leap for joy when we find someone who appreciates God's Word," she said, pointing out Matthew 5:6: "Blessed are they which do hunger and thirst after righteousness: for they shall be filled."

"Everlasting life depends on knowledge and understanding of God's Word and doing His will," she wrote.

That's what I wanted—to please God so that He would be proud of me. I longed to be worthy of being with my kids again.

"Would you like someone to come to your house and discuss the Bible with you?" she asked. "If you would, let me know, and I will arrange for someone to visit you. I only wish I were close enough to have that privilege myself."

Enclosed with the letter was a magazine that told me what God planned to do for the earth and humanity. I wrote back to Mrs. Brents that I would love to have someone study with me.

The Christmas season came, and with it the quiet loneliness of a childless home. We decorated a tree as usual, but without tinsel, for there were no small hands to toss it in clumps around the room. Memories of joyful Christmases past filled in the solitary times of the present. To satisfy my desire to have toys under the Christmas tree I bought my husband a train set, complete with little trees and bushes, signs and power poles, and old-fashioned buildings.

George was still working nights, and I still kept my schedule to his, though I realized that when the baby was born I'd have to adjust it again. I didn't mind his working such odd hours now, but I hoped he would find a daytime job before the baby arrived. He offered to trade shifts with another security man for Christmas day. The man had children, and we both agreed that it would be nice to let him share Christmas with his family. Since we had no children, we could "celebrate" anytime.

On Christmas Eve we opened our presents, just the two of us. We were so used to hearing the kids run into the bedroom just before sunrise yelling "Is it time yet?" that we didn't know how to start. Usually we had to hold them off till I got the coffee going for George. When we finally did give the OK they began reading tags at 90 miles an hour and distributing packages just as fast.

It was different now.

"Are you ready to open presents?" I finally asked.

"Oh, I guess. You want to go first?"

"Naw, why don't you go first."

"Go ahead. You can be first."

It's amazing that we ever got started at all!

One day a pleasant young woman knocked on my

door and introduced herself as Marla. Since she already knew my name, I realized that she must be the woman that Mrs. Brents had offered to send to study the Bible with me. I welcomed her into my home. We talked for a short time to get to know each other before settling down to study.

Marla knew that the subject I was most interested in was death and the resurrection. She gave me a small hardbound book about eternal life and offered to help me understand what the Bible said about the topic. I opened my Bible and fumbled through it to find the scriptures she suggested, but I had never hunted a specific text before. I found it difficult and time consuming. Patiently Marla began teaching me how to memorize the order of the books.

"Genesis, Exodus, Leviticus," I recited.

Marla came to my house twice a week, and with each visit I memorized the names of a few more of the books in the Bible.

"Matthew, Mark, Luke, and John are the four Gospels, or the good news of Christ," she explained. "Then come Acts, Romans, and Corinthians."

With time I became more familiar with my Bible and more confident in looking up the verses. I was thrilled with my new knowledge and impressed with how much this young woman knew. Filled with questions, I looked forward to her visits.

But as we studied further I started to doubt some of the things she told me. We were beginning to depend more on her books and magazines than on Scripture itself, and when I looked in the Bible to verify her answers, it didn't seem to clearly indicate what she said. Sometimes I noticed that she left out the verses before and after in order to make her point, and that didn't seem right.

Marla believed that only a special group numbering 144,000 would go to heaven. Common people like us would inherit the earth and never actually live in heaven. That puzzled me. Why would God play favorites? Had the quota already been met? Could the special group visit the commoners? Certainly the commoners couldn't go visit those in heaven. What if I outdid myself in my search and reached the higher goal? Then I'd never see my kids again. It was a very real concern to me. The thought of living eternally on earth or in heaven was only secondary. Most important was my need to be with my children again.

I read in some of the publications that Marla gave me that Jesus had already returned back in 1914. Why? If He had already come back, then why was there still so much evil in the world? Jesus told His disciples that He would return to receive them unto Himself. If He had already done that, why were my kids still in the grave? How many times was He going to come back, anyway? The more I thought about it the less sense it made. I cut our studies down to once a week and studied the Bible more on my own. Somehow, I would figure all this out. I was not studying the Bible out of some simple curiosity. For me, my search had become a quest for truth.

On January 23, 1978, a preliminary hearing was held for Billy Dyer and Ray Richardson in

Camdenton, Missouri. It presented a statement that Richardson had written to the police after his arrest, stating that Billy had told him repeatedly that he planned to steal several guns and knives from the Swift home while the parents were away and that "if he had to kill them [the children] he would in order to get them."

Debbie Balentine testified that on the night of the murders she received a phone call from Stephanie, who asked her to relay a message to her parents. The girl drove to our home and saw that three of the children were either badly injured or dead. Terrified, she went to a neighbor's house to summon the police.

Trooper Herb Thomas testified that he inquired at the Camdenton Junior High School after the murders to see if he could find out anything about the Swift boys. Two students told him they had heard Billy Dyer say that he would steal guns from the Swift home and that he would kill to do it. Both boys testified at the hearing that Billy often talked at school about stealing the guns and some knives. One classmate testified that Billy had claimed that if anybody got in the way he'd take care of them. The boys quoted Billy as saying on the morning of the murders that he couldn't wait to open fire on the children and get the guns. Both boys said that Billy had told them he would give them guns or knives if they kept quiet about his plans. Neither of them had believed he would actually do it.

When the boys learned that our children had been murdered they went to their school counselor, who took them to the principal. They later repeated their story to Trooper Thomas in the presence of a juvenile officer.

In closing, Billy's attorney argued that Billy's constitutional right to confront a witness against him had been violated when Richardson's statement was read in the hearing. He moved for dismissal of the charges. Richardson's attorney pointed out that no physical evidence had been taken at the scene of the crime to indicate that Richardson had been there, and he also moved for dismissal.

The judge denied both motions to dismiss and ordered both defendants bound over for trial, charged with four counts of capital murder. The penalty for this crime was either life imprisonment with no parole for 50 years, or the death penalty.

I didn't want the boys to get the death penalty. Someone had told me that God, being merciful, could forgive them if they repented, and would then allow them into heaven. I didn't want them in heaven so soon. My kids had just gotten there! Instead, I wanted them to be punished and suffer for what they had done. Besides, if Marla was right and the dead simply slept in the grave, that also was too easy for them. Someday they would stand before God, but for now I intended for them to experience a living hell on earth. They needed to know fear in prison—fear without any chance for escape like my kids had felt. I wanted no mercy, for they had shown none.

I dreamed of visiting them in their cells with a long chain. There I'd whip them ceaselessly as they cowered beside the jail bunks. I envisioned gangs of prisoners surrounding them and no one hearing their cries. I wanted them thrown into a dark, windowless cell, never to see the sunshine again.

But I didn't want them dead. Not yet.

A formal arraignment hearing was held for Billy Dyer on February 10. He pled "Not guilty by reason of mental defect excluding responsibility for his conduct." The judge granted his attorney's request that Billy be psychiatrically examined. Billy remained in custody without bond, pending a trial.

On September 8, 1978, Billy waived his right to a jury trial that had been scheduled for the eighteenth of that same month. On a change of venue, he went before the Johnson County Circuit Judge to try to plea bargain. He pled guilty of first-degree murder in the deaths of Greg and Steve. The judge accepted his plea, dismissing the charges against him in Tonya and Stacy's deaths.

It made me furious. Billy had killed all four of my children, and I wanted him punished for all four murders. He had not tried to plea bargain with my kids. Dyer could have had the guns without the violence. He knew where we kept them. If he had stolen the pistols one by one, we probably wouldn't even have missed them for a while.

I despised the judge for accepting Billy's pleas, until I realized that he set the punishment at the harshest level possible for both murders.

Billy Dyer was sentenced on both counts to imprisonment in the Department of Corrections of the State of Missouri for the rest of his natural life. The two life sentences were to run consecutively, not concurrently.

We contacted our attorney to ask when Billy would be eligible for parole. He answered by letter, saying, "For a simple life sentence there is no parole for 10 years. In this case, a multiple sentence, it will take a considerable period of time before this defendant is eligible for parole."

# SANDY

The strike at the construction company where George worked finally ended, eliminating the need for security at the building. However, the same company offered him a welding job and he started the day shift. We began to eat days and sleep nights like normal people.

In early April, as I entered my fifth month of pregnancy, I started to hemorrhage. Not badly the first day, but by the third it had increased to the point that it alarmed me. I visited Dr. Horseman and asked what was wrong. He said that if we didn't take steps to prevent it, I might lose the baby. I had never seen him look this concerned. Tears burned in my eyes.

"Dr. Horseman," I pleaded, "I can't lose number six. I'm not strong enough to bury another child."

"We don't have to lose it," he said compassionately. "I'm going to give you a shot that will help prevent a miscarriage. If there is something wrong with a baby it usually miscarries in the first trimester. I want you to go to bed, and stay there. And call me if the bleeding gets worse."

I went directly home and stayed in bed. George made sure that everything was within reach so I wouldn't need to get up. He was very quiet that evening, and I didn't realize how scared he was. The next day he went privately to talk to the doctor. While he was afraid I would lose the baby, he was even more terrified that there might be something wrong with the baby, a handicap that he couldn't deal with. If that was the case, he didn't want the doctor to attempt to save the child but to let it miscarry. We could try to have another one later, a healthy one.

Dr. Horseman assured him that had a deformity in the baby caused the bleeding, I would probably have miscarried already in spite of anything he could do. The biggest cause for the bleeding was that the opening of the cervix hadn't had a chance to heal properly before the pressure of pregnancy was placed upon it. If I stayed in bed and kept the pressure off the cervix, everything should be fine.

My husband came home and told me about his visit with the doctor.

"I was really scared," he said. "That's why I had to talk with him alone. But I'm OK now. It's all going to work out."

For three weeks I stayed in bed, and the bleeding quit as long as I remained lying down.

Marla continued to come for our studies, but by my second week in bed I decided I didn't want to continue with her anymore. She phoned and I put her off. Then she stopped by, and I told her that the doctor had confined me to bed. When she offered to sit beside my bed and study with me, I said that George didn't want me to have company.

The real reason was that she had presented too many things I couldn't verify in the Bible. A sincere woman, she honestly believed what she told me, and she only wanted to share her hope and joy with me. I appreciated that, but I was confused and I felt that I should work it out myself. At the same time I realized that with so many churches in the world it could take a very long time to find the right one. They couldn't all be right. God just couldn't be that flexible. There had to be one true answer, and surely there was some-one out there that had it. I decided to search alone for a while, to figure it out myself.

To make matters worse, my Mom had begun to read several books about reincarnation. The concept of past lives fascinated her, and she imagined that surely she had once been an Arabian princess or some such thing. She told me that our present lives are designed to teach us lessons not learned in previous ones. For instance, she said that Tonya may have been my mother in a past life and we may not have related to one another well, so she returned as my daughter to learn that lesson. I resented that. Mom and I never did fully understand each other. We were so different. But I had a good relationship with my daughter. Granted, Tonya was still young. Those teen years would have been the big test. Perhaps Tonya died young, Mom suggested, because she had learned the lesson and was prepared for a new life. She was now somebody else altogether, learning another lesson. Eventually her character would be completely per-fected. Mom didn't know quite what was supposed to happen after that, though.

One of her books suggested that babies have a

one-year probationary period to decide if the parents to whom they have been assigned will teach them the particular lesson to be learned. If the parents prove to be inadequate, the child may choose to leave. This, the book claimed, is the cause of the sudden infant death syndrome. Such babies would receive a new identity and return to the earth as different persons with different parents.

I could not accept this bizarre teaching at all. It shocked me that Mom would even consider such a concept. Tonya was my daughter, given to me by God. She had never been anyone else's daughter before. The thing that hurt me the worst about this belief was that I was trying with all my might to find the way to heaven. If I finally reached that goal only to discover that Tonya had been sent back to earth to be someone else, I would be extremely angry. No one could ever love her as I had. How could anyone ever have any real feelings of identity and self-worth if they kept becoming different people? Loving my children for what they were and who they were, I didn't want them to be anyone else. Besides, if I was reincarnated and became a peasant somewhere and my kids became other individuals, my family would be spread around the globe, and I would never have any hope of bringing us all together. I'd spend my whole new life searching for a familiar trait that would reveal that some stranger was once my son. While such ideas gave Mom much happiness that Tonya was alive out there somewhere, the same thoughts destroyed all my hopes to reunite my family again someday.

My hemorrhaging stopped a month after it began, and with caution the doctor gave me permission to live normally again. The rest of the pregnancy was uneventful.

My due date was set for August 1, but when the day came and went without a single labor pain, a great depression set in. Having waited so long to hold this baby, I felt that I couldn't wait another minute longer. I lay around the house like a beached whale, blubbering in despair. On the third of August I thought I was in labor, but a visit to the doctor's office dispelled my hopes. It was a false alarm. Leaving the office, I found it impossible to hold back the tears. George did his best to soothe me, but I would not be comforted.

Finally I went into labor on August 5. There was no doubt this time! I called Dr. Horseman at 3:00 p.m., and he told us to head for the hospital. I was so excited. Labor was always easy for me. In a few short hours I would be holding my baby.

George stayed with me to time the pains. Shortly before 6:00 I asked him to get a nurse, because I felt the need to push. He turned pale, scared to death I'd have the baby while he was in the room. "They built that nice father's waiting room," he always said, "and it's the least I can do to use it." My husband ran out into the hall to find a nurse.

The nurse came in to check my progress and discovered that I was fully dilated. "We'd better get you into delivery right now," she announced.

George was in the hall as they wheeled me quickly toward the delivery room. "You all right?" he asked.

"Yeah, this won't take long," I answered confidently. "I can already feel the baby's head."

Dr. Horseman barely had time to put on his gloves. "Don't push yet!" he shouted through two contractions, then readied himself for the third and gave me the OK.

"You've got a beautiful baby girl!" he announced at exactly 6:00 as he placed the tiny infant on my belly.

"She's such a pretty baby!" the nurse exclaimed. "Do you have a name picked out for her?"

"Sandy Dey Swift," I said proudly as I caressed my daughter's velvety skin.

After bathing, weighing, and measuring the baby, the nurse wrapped her in a pink blanket and laid her beside me. We were wheeled out together to be reunited with George.

A nurse checked my vital signs regularly to make sure that everything returned to normal after delivery. Absolutely exhausted even though the labor and delivery room had been a breeze, I kept dozing off.

It was well into the night when the nurse discovered that I was hemorrhaging again. She phoned Dr. Horseman to return to the hospital. He called George to tell him to come as well. I was surprised to see the doctor when he arrived. By now I was really drowsy and couldn't think straight. I was losing too much blood. Dr. Horseman, a big man, placed both hands on my stomach and pushed with great might to expel any remaining afterbirth and clots of blood. The pain was excruciating. Grabbing his wrist and wrenching his watchband, I tried to make him ease up on the pressure. He looked really concerned. Dr. Horseman knew it hurt, and he had never hurt me before. But I trusted him. Although I knew he was only doing what had to be done, I still couldn't bear the pain.

A nurse brought in a pint of blood and quickly piggybacked it into an IV of normal saline. I felt the chilled blood enter my hand and turn my veins cold. George entered and stayed until the nurse thought they had the bleeding under control, then returned home to get some sleep.

The sun was coming up when they transferred me to a regular room upstairs, the pint of blood still dripping slowly into my veins. I had not eaten since breakfast Saturday, and I was absolutely starving. They brought me a sandwich and juice. As I wolfed down the first enormous bite my stomach growled. I was still very drowsy, and kept dozing off between bites. Then I'd wake to find I still had food in my mouth, but I refused to give up until I had eaten every last bite. I slept soundly, my eyes blinking only when the nurse periodically checked my vital signs. When breakfast was served a few hours later I felt great. The IV was gone.

A new hospital policy offered an early bonding experience for fathers. George scrubbed meticulously under the watchful eye of a stern nurse and then obediently donned a ridiculous knee-length gown. I had to chuckle when he entered my room with his mountain man physique wearing a silly feminine gown. He carried in his hand a vase full of pink roses.

A nurse brought Sandy's bassinet, and George looked anxiously at her.

"Go ahead and pick her up," I prodded.

Bending over the bassinet, he awkwardly took up his daughter. He sat in the chair beside the bed, holding her protectively, admiring her nonchalant little grin, talking softly to her. How could any harm ever come to this child with those big arms to protect her?

The pediatrician came in later to report that Sandy had jaundice. Tonya and Stacy had both had jaundice, and I was not overly concerned about it, but I learned that their jaundice had been only at level two. Sandy's was at level six. They told me they would put her under a special light that would correct the problem. Again, I thought little about it.

My second evening at the hospital my parents came to see me. Mom decided to walk down the hall and see Sandy through the nursery window. She came back quite tickled, saying, "Oh Joy, you ought to see Sandy. They've got her under the light. She's got a little mask on, and she's kicking her tiny feet. She looks so cute."

Slipping on my robe, I went with Mom to see my daughter. What I saw appalled me. My tiny child was in a bassinet completely undressed. A mask covered her eyes and wrapped around her head. It looked as if it was made of tape. The thought hit me that when they took off the mask it would pull her tender skin and peach-fuzz hair. I envisioned her screaming in pain. Her knees and heels were already rubbed raw from kicking. She was crying under the intense light, and no nurse stood by to comfort her. A glass barrier kept me from her. Horrified at what they were doing to my innocent baby, I returned to my room and demanded that someone explain what they were doing to my child.

A nurse matter-of-factly proceeded to tell me what the special light was for. She demonstrated a mask identical to the one Sandy was wearing. Made of felt and velcro, it could in no way hurt her. The mask protected her eyes from the bright light. Much to my surprise she further explained that newborns do not like to be naked. Accustomed to being cradled in a womb surrounded by warm fluid, they enjoy the security of that warmth. That is why, when a newborn is fussy, they wrap it tightly in a blanket to give it a sense of security. Sandy felt insecure because she had to be naked under the light, so she kicked to try to curl up into a ball.

On the third day Dr. Horseman approved my release, but Sandy had to stay for another day of treatment under the light. When we finally took her home, Sandy could have won an award for the most cuddled baby. George and I spent every conceivable moment holding her, studying her features, and comparing them to the other kids. Although we saw in her a little bit of each of them, she most favored Stephanie. We talked to her about how much her brothers and sisters would have loved her. Greg would have given her a bottle of juice and rocked her. Stacy would have counted her little toes. Reveling in the sound of our voices, Sandy kicked her tiny feet. It didn't matter that she couldn't understand what we said. What mattered was that we always had something to talk about.

Not a day went by that we didn't think about the kids. I dreamed of them every night, fantasizing that they would come home. I dreamed of camping trips and playing games. I dreamed that it was all a hoax. They hadn't really died. Those bodies were dummies. My children were alive, and I discovered it, and got them back. I spent my days caring for Sandy and loving every minute of it. But I looked forward to nightfall so that I could dream about the other kids and pretend that I was with them. I lived my life in two shifts, the conscious and unconscious. Whenever my grief began to get the best of me I would lie down and dream that the kids were with me again. I wore a gold band bracelet with all five names engraved in it and a big gold cross around my neck to connect me with heaven where the kids were "safe in the arms of Jesus."

When Sandy was three weeks old we moved to a little house across from a huge Catholic church and school. As I watched the children walking to school each morning I considered how nice it would be for Sandy to go there when she was old enough. I could watch her from my big picture window until she reached the school doors. I didn't ever want to let her out of my sight for fear that she wouldn't be there when I came back.

# MY CATHOLIC FRIENDS

I got to know our neighbors mainly through their children. When I asked them how they liked going to Catholic schools as opposed to public schools, they all answered positively. I could see by their attitude that the discipline wasn't hurting them any. Their assuredness in religious matters impressed me. They knew that God watched over them.

I became especially close to the Madden family next door. They had six children, and over the next year I nearly adopted Pat, who was 12 years old and so much like Greg and Steve. He and his little brother Paul were over constantly, and I loved it. I became very popular with many of the neighbor kids, and Sandy had lots of foster brothers and sisters to keep her content. I welcomed their visits with open arms. Every one of them was polite and respectful. The way their parents were raising them and the values they learned through the Catholic school greatly impressed me. I wanted Sandy to grow up like that. These kids were a great influence on me.

George and I talked a lot about our neighbors and started discussing the Catholic Church. My husband had wanted to become a Catholic during his service in the Air Force. Fascinated by its beauty, he had attended mass regularly for a while. But after getting out of the service he compromised and attended the Episcopal Church.

My own family had attended an Episcopal church when I was in the sixth grade. My 8-year-old cousin was dying of leukemia, and my aunt and uncle had started going to church. My parents followed suit, although not regularly. I never went to Sunday school. After Crystal died Mom put my brother and me in the car and said, "We're going to church to have you baptized."

"What for?" we wanted to know.

"It won't hurt. The priest is just going to sprinkle some water on your head, say a few words, and we can go home."

The priest was the only one there. It was not a public celebration. Neither Rick nor I understood why we were being baptized, but it was done and over with. I can only assume that Mom took Dawn and Jack another day to have them baptized.

My aunt and uncle quit going to church after they buried Crystal. My uncle blamed God for taking away his little girl. "A loving and merciful God wouldn't do that," he said. My family quit going as well, so our church-attending days ended almost as quickly as they began.

The more I thought about how I had grown up, the more I wanted Sandy to experience what I had missed and what I was still searching for. The neighborhood children told me Bible stories that I had never heard, such as Daniel in the lions' den and the youths thrown in the fiery furnace who yet remained unharmed. God is there when His people need Him.

These kids were sure of that.

During the following months we continued to observe and consider the church across the street.

Ray Richardson's trial resulted in a lenient sentence for him, upsetting me greatly. I started to hemorrhage again. Several visits to the doctor failed to clear up the problem. The doctor even tried to cauterize the cervical opening to stop the bleeding, but that didn't work either. Finally he asked, "Have you tried going to church?"

It surprised me. My mind had been on church a lot lately, but his question really motivated me. I talked to my husband that evening about what the doctor had said. George went alone the next day to talk with the priest. Some confirmation classes would start in a few weeks. After George returned home we discussed the classes, and I agreed it would be good for both of us to attend. Visiting the priest myself, I told him about the kids's deaths, about all the questions I still had about death and heaven, and how impressed I was with the neighborhood children. He acted as if he was proud of the children in the school, as if he were also a part of them. By the time I returned home I was pretty happy.

It felt good to be finally moving ahead. This church just had to be right. I looked forward to the classes.

The neighborhood girls took turns baby-sitting Sandy during the evening sessions. Sandy was usually in bed by 7:00, before we even left the house. Because we were only across the street and the whole neighborhood stuck together like a big family, we knew that she would be safe.

George and I really enjoyed the fellowship of our classmates. We took turns bringing a dessert, and the informal meetings were a lot of fun. I read my lessons diligently, eager to learn as much as I could.

When we reached the subject of death, though, I hit a snag. The priest told me that since Tonya and Stacy had not been baptized, they were now in a place called limbo until they could learn more about Christ and reach heaven. I just couldn't accept that. It was my fault that they had not been baptized. Surely God wouldn't keep them out of heaven just because I had failed to have them sprinkled with water. Then I thought of my own baptism, how meaningless and uneventful it had seemed to me. How could such an insignificant event—or the lack of it—have had any impact on my baby girls? I just didn't understand this at all. The priest also indicated that Billy Dyer, if he'd been baptized, had a better chance of attaining heaven than the girls he had killed! This blew my mind. What kind of God was He? I just couldn't accept such a teaching at all.

I told myself that Tonya and Stacy were in heaven with the other three kids. God would not separate them like that. Still I prayed and felt wretched about it for months, asking God to punish me for failing to live up to my responsibility as a parent. I begged Him to let my babies into heaven. It was my fault. I would pay the price for them. "Send *me* to limbo. Send *me* to hell if You want, but let my children be with You in heaven." I shed many tears as I tried to come up with ways to atone for my irresponsibility so my girls would definitely go to heaven, but regardless of how much I begged God, I was never sure if He heard.

We continued with the confirmation classes, though George began to lose interest before they were over and didn't study his lessons as he should have. I kept studying and filled him in before each class so that he would know what was going on.

As we studied, we learned about the sacrament of marriage. George and I decided that we would like to renew our vows in a ceremony in the church, and planned to do so on September 11, our wedding anniversary.

Sandy's baptism was scheduled a few weeks later. She was baptized with three other infants, all younger than she. Sandy was now 1 year old. The others were tiny babies. It was a solemn occasion. I was not going to make the same mistake with Sandy that I had made with Tonya and Stacy. I still felt wretched over my failure to have them baptized, and I was still trying to atone for it any way I could.

Now I was a Catholic, a member of a big family, and I felt as if I belonged. I went to confession and did penance for certain past sins that I had committed while a teenager. It felt good to have this filth erased from my record. No longer would I have to carry my past around with me. I was starting out new, clean and white, and I vowed to stay that way. I didn't want to do anything that would make me ashamed if God saw it. To my surprise, after nearly nine months, the hemorrhaging stopped.

# ELEVEN

# MATTHEW AND MICHAEL

The first of January, 1980, an old familiar feeling began to invade my mornings. It didn't surprise me at all to learn that I was pregnant once again. The baby was due the first of September.

By now we were into the routine of attending mass. I had all the prayers and songs pretty well memorized, but I never did go to confession again. I never felt that I did anything to warrant it. A good wife and mother and an honest person, I had nothing to be sorry for. I quit looking for answers in the Bible, concentrating instead on learning the different parts of the mass and other Catholic teachings. I believed that I was living a godly life each day and that this would earn me my right to be with my kids again.

By the middle of my pregnancy the job situation was so bad that we decided to return to the Ozarks. The move proved to be the end of our relationship with the Catholic Church except for a service now and then, but I will always look back on that part of my life as a time of spiritual growth and real joy. The Catholic Church made a lasting impression on my life, for which I shall ever be thankful and which I shall never forget.

The area around the Lake of the Ozarks held too many painful memories. Since we couldn't go back there, we headed farther south to the Table Rock Lake area just north of the Arkansas-Missouri border. There we moved into a rustic log cabin several hundred yards from the lake. The beach was of fine sand, just perfect for Sandy to play in. We bought her a life vest, and she loved to paddle around in the shallows. I spent the summer in the water to keep cool. It was a very hot summer, and my added insulation made me miserable. As long as I was in the lake I felt comfortable.

We had to make regular trips back to Kansas City for my prenatal visits. Dr. Horseman said it was still possible for me to deliver in Kansas City, if I had relatives to stay with when the time drew near, so the last few weeks we spent a lot of time at my parents' house.

The evening of August 29 I went into labor. We left for the hospital at precisely midnight. By now the pains were quite regular and close together, but I wasn't really uncomfortable. Our son was born at 1:57 a.m. on August 30. We named him Matthew Thomas Swift, or little M. T., after George's dad.

Matthew was 100 percent a Swift. He had all the family traits of the other kids. He weighed in at seven pounds, six-and-a-half ounces—my biggest baby to date. To my relief, he showed no signs of jaundice. Nobody was going to keep me from taking this baby home on time!

When Matthew was only three days old we returned home to our Ozark cabin. The nights turned nippy as September came, and we enjoyed the crisp Indian summer days. When Matthew was three weeks old I tucked him into the front bib of my overalls, and we took a family hike in the woods each day. I enjoyed my newfound freedom to roam with the family. We spent many hours on the beach together looking for arrowheads. Often George would watch the kids at naptime so I could go by myself to the woods. The peacefulness of being totally alone in the great outdoors soothes the soul. I relished the sounds of the wind in the trees and the waves licking up onto the shore and the crisp gurgle of a trickling stream moving freely down the creek bed. I envied the water for its freedom.

Christmas was something special that year. I made lots of wooden toys for the kids and more wooden gifts for all the relatives. The only store-bought toy was a big red wagon. It was an old-fashioned, home-made Christmas, but that didn't matter to Sandy. She squealed with delight at each present. Matthew cooed and cried and grinned and tried to eat the bows. Later in the day, while the kids napped, George and I went outside to cut some firewood. The aroma of hickory smoke wafted from the chimney. Light flakes began to fall from the afternoon sky. They stuck to our eyelids. It was a beautiful day, and we were content to be living here all alone with no one to bother us or push their lifestyle onto us.

Had it not been for the economy we would never have left our Ozarks home. Jobs were nonexistent, and we just couldn't hold on any longer. In February we left our little paradise and returned to Kansas. George secured a job in Clay Center. A few months later we moved to Manhattan, Kansas, where he began working for the University of Kansas in the Agronomy Department. He enjoyed his work that kept him outdoors most of the time, planting and harvesting, cultivating, and hoeing the acres of experimental crops.

We rented a small house in the country surrounded by wheat fields. I liked it much better than living in town. And I was pregnant again. The baby was due in August, just like Sandy and Matt. I don't know how I managed that. It just happened.

With George working, it seemed impractical to try to have this baby delivered by Dr. Horseman, so I found an obstetrician in Wamego who worked out of the little hospital there.

I went into labor on August 21, 1982. The pains were nothing drastic, and I was having an easy time of it. When I arrived at the hospital at 8:00 p.m. I was taken to the birthing room. This would be a new experience. The nurses hooked me up to a machine that monitored my contractions. Amazed by it, George watched as the needle rose to a peak and then gently fell back down.

"You're having another pain. Here it comes," he would announce.

"No kidding," I'd answer sarcastically. "I can feel it from my end."

The doctor asked my husband if he planned to stay for the birthing.

"Oh, no," he said. "I'll just wait outside till it's over." He stood by the door the last few minutes while the doctor checked my progress.

"You can push with the next pain if you want," the

physician told me.

I looked toward the door. My husband had disappeared.

Two pushes later, Michael was born. It was almost 10:00. George came back in then, huddling near the wall to avoid what was going on a few feet away. A nurse brought Michael over to the table to be measured, and George turned his attention to his son. After the nurse cleaned him up, she asked my husband if he would like to carry the baby down the hall to be weighed. George was elated. When he returned with Michael he absolutely beamed with pride.

"Guess how much he weighs," he exclaimed.

"Seven pounds, fourteen ounces," I replied.

"Nope. He weighs eight pounds, two and a half ounces."

I couldn't believe it. I never thought I'd have a baby more than eight pounds.

Michael's homecoming was a great event. Sandy and Matt were so excited. Daddy sat protectively on the couch while they took turns holding their new baby brother. I watched them silently, soaking up the moment, glowing with pride and satisfaction. It had been a rough pregnancy for me —such a hot summer—and I was glad that it was over. Now that the children outnumbered the parents, I was beginning to feel like a real family again. But past memories began to creep into our wonderful day.

Tears blurred my vision as I recalled Stacy's homecoming and how excited Steve, Greg, and Tonya had been. How abruptly that happiness had ended five years ago, when all of them were killed. We never used the word died when we referred to them, because none of them had simply died on their own. Left to themselves they all would have lived. They were all struck down, four by bullets, one by cancer.

George and I had definite plans for our three new children. We felt that we just had to get back to the land, to eliminate as many outside influences on their lives as possible. He and I were afraid for our children. Afraid that this cruel world would continue to prey upon our little ones. I believe that if George and I had thought it even remotely possible, we would have just taken our family underground and raised them there alone where nobody could find and harm us. We had not had a baby-sitter since we left the Catholic neighborhood, fearing that if we left the kids with anyone something terrible would happen while we were gone. Only occasionally would we drop them by George's mother so we could go do some birthday shopping or such, but they were quite a handful for a woman now in her eighties. Because we went virtually everywhere as a family, we decided that it was time to quit having babies and start raising the ones we had.

Michael's birth brought a renewed desire to seek God once more. Matthew was 2 years old, and he still wasn't baptized. Now we had another son in need of baptism. I felt almost like a failure. It was my fault that Tonya and Stacy had never been baptized. They had been killed before they ever had a chance to be. It frightened me that the same thing might happen to my two young sons. Constantly I lived with the fear of death. If death did strike again, my family was not prepared spiritually for that. Such thoughts filled my mind for weeks. Finally I decided to attend the Catholic church again.

I went alone that first Sunday. Although I had invited George, he declined. After mass I stayed to talk with the priest. He was very kind, and I liked him. I told him about my children's deaths and how we had found the Catholic Church, but I couldn't bring myself to tell him that Matt had not been baptized. I didn't feel quite so guilty about Michael because he was still so small. But I didn't mention him either.

After that I attended mass regularly by myself. George just didn't want to go. I left the kids with him so that I could concentrate. I enjoyed the mass, even partaking of the Holy Eucharist, though I knew I shouldn't when I was hiding the facts about the boys. It weighed heavily on my conscience and made me feel ashamed. I didn't know how to take this problem directly to God. I thought I had to take it to the priest in the confessional, but I just couldn't bring myself to do it. Instead, I got out my rosary and said the prayers around the beads, trying to gain some courage, but without success. I wanted with all my heart to do right by my children. They were my whole life, all that was important to me. My other live were some-how in the hands of God, though I still wasn't certain just how. I wanted desperately to be close to Him. But right now I felt very far away.

# TWELVE

# THE ANSWERS START COMING

I had never realized how much the deaths of my children had affected my sister, Dawn. Now married with a baby girl of her own, she too had been searching for answers. One day she received a letter in the mail offering free Bible study guides. She responded to the offer out of curiosity and soon began to receive the Voice of Prophecy lessons in the mail. The Bible was her only textbook, the guides leading her through it a subject at a time. One day she came with my parents on a visit. We went shopping alone so we could talk.

Dawn opened the conversation by asking if I was still going to church and studying the Bible. I told her I had just started attending mass again, but that I hadn't picked up my Bible in a long time.

She thought a moment. "I want to talk to you about something," she said at last. "There are some things I've learned that I feel I must tell you, but I'm afraid you'll be offended."

"Dawn, the only thing that matters to me is the truth," I said. "I've got to be with my kids again. That's my main goal. If I ever find out that I've been wrong, I'll gladly change. Go ahead and tell me."

"Are you sure?"

"I'm sure."

"Well, a few months ago I started getting these Voice of Prophecy lessons in the mail. I began doing them, and they were lots of fun, but I learned some things that I've got to tell you." She held her breath.

"What is it, Dawn?" I asked.

She turned to me. "Do you believe your kids are in heaven, or asleep in the graves until Jesus comes again?"

"You mean you can answer that question for me, Dawn? From the Bible?"

"Yes."

"Dawn, that's the answer I've been looking for! Some people say the kids are in heaven. Others say they're in a place called limbo till they learn more. Mom's told me that maybe they've been reincarnated into somebody else, and that about blows my mind. It seems that everybody has a different opinion about where they are. The last time I saw them they were ready to be lowered into a grave. It's all been very confusing to me. All I want to know is which one is right."

"The Bible doesn't talk about limbo," Dawn said. "Jesus said 'Suffer the little children to come unto me, for of such is the kingdom of heaven' [Matthew 19:14]. He wouldn't keep them out. But it also says that the dead are asleep."

"But where?" I demanded.

"When Lazarus died, Jesus said that he was asleep [John 11:10]. Another place says that the living know that they will die, but the dead don't know anything [Ecclesiastes 9:5]. The body returns to the dust."

"But not the soul," I challenged.

"'The soul that sinneth, it shall die' [Ezekiel 18:4]. And according to the Bible every human being is a sinner."

I couldn't believe what I was hearing. "So you're saying that the soul dies too?" I asked incredulously.

My sister nodded. "The soul is the whole person. God breathed into Adam the breath of life, and he became a living soul [Genesis 2:7]. The Creator didn't *give* him a soul. Adam *became* a soul."

"So you're saying that when you die every part of you dies? You just sleep in the grave till Jesus comes to raise you up?"

"Yes. There are a whole bunch more verses in the Bible to prove it. Think about it. If people go to heaven when they die, why is Jesus coming back to raise them?"

I considered that a minute. It made sense. I'd have to study it for myself, of course. "OK, I can handle that," I said. "What else did you learn?"

"About baptism."

That was a subject that had been worrying me a lot. "What about it?" My words were almost as much a demand as a question.

"You don't need to worry about Tonya and Stacy. There is nothing in the Bible about infant baptism."

I breathed a sigh of relief.

"The Bible says you should be immersed in water, not sprinkled," Dawn continued. "It also says, 'Go ye therefore and teach all nations, baptizing them' [Matthew 28:19]. You teach them first. You can't teach a newborn baby about God. Tonya and Stacy weren't old enough to know."

"Is that true?"

"When was Jesus baptized?" Dawn questioned. "Was He a baby?"

I thought a minute. "No, He was grown."

"And didn't He set an example for us?"

"Yes."

"How many babies did John the Baptist baptize?"

"None that I know of."

"You see?"

"Do you mean that I've been miserable about my babies not being baptized all these years for nothing?"

"I guess so," Dawn said quietly.

My sister told me that she had become a Seventh-day Adventist. I remembered the nurse who comforted me at the hospital in Kansas City after my cancer surgery. Dawn said that she especially liked the Sabbath school program for the children.

"What's Sabbath school?" I asked.

"Just like Sunday school, but it's not on Sunday so you can't call it Sunday school," she explained.

"If you don't go to church on Sunday, when do you go?"

"On Saturday."

"But, why?"

"Because the fourth commandment says, 'Remember the Sabbath day to keep it holy' [Exodus 20:8]."

"How do you know that Saturday is the Sabbath?" I questioned.

"The Bible says that the Sabbath is the seventh day

of the week [Exodus 20:10]. If you look on the calendar, Saturday is the seventh day."

"You're right," I said, rather confused.

"At Sabbath school they begin teaching the children about Jesus and the stories from the Bible even before they're old enough to walk!"

"Really?" That intrigued me.

"Yeah, and Darcy loves it."

"I'd like to see those Voice of Prophecy lessons for myself. Where can I get them?"

"I'll lend you mine," Dawn replied. "But I do want them back. Mom and Dad are coming back here in a few weeks. I'll bring them then."

For three weeks I kept my conversation with her to myself, realizing that George would not understand my interest. I thought about it during the quiet hours of the night, asking God to guide me. If I was wrong I requested that He show me the correct way. I sincerely wanted to do what was right.

When Dawn returned with my parents she carried the study guides in a yellow folder. She and Darcy recited a few of the songs and finger plays they had learned in Sabbath school. It touched my heart to see a 2-year-old sing about Jesus. Again we went off alone to talk.

I told my sister that I had serious doubts about my faith that I felt I must confront immediately. I must know the truth. As Dawn left that evening we promised to keep in touch. I wished that we lived closer to each other so we could study together. And I admired her enthusiasm, her confidence, her spiritual zeal. It was a side of her I had never seen before, a side that I once had but had let dwindle away.

Once I had searched diligently, asking questions of anyone who might know, who might lead me closer to spiritual truth. But I no longer felt like that, and I missed it. Simply going to mass was not enough. I must begin to study the Scriptures once more. Suddenly I realized that I had absolutely no idea where my Bible was. I must find it.

That evening after the kids were tucked into bed I decided it was time to tell George a little bit about what my sister had told me. Careful not to criticize the Catholic Church, I explained how impressed I was with Dawn's enthusiasm, something I missed in myself.

"I think it's great that Dawn found God in her church," he replied. "But you found God in the Catholic Church. I don't mind if you take some lessons, but if you're going to do it, write to the Knights of Columbus and get some Catholic ones. I'm not criticizing Dawn. But we are Catholics, and there's plenty of Catholic literature out there. Just let me know what you want, and we'll get it for you."

By the time he was finished I was convinced he was probably right and agreed to the Catholic lessons. I had never gone against my husband in my life.

That night I lay awake communing with God, searching my soul, and reorganizing my priorities. I prayed earnestly for Him to lead me in the right direction now. George lay peacefully beside me. I loved him so very much. But the words Dawn said to me kept coming back. She made sense. I needed to know what was right. After wrestling with my thoughts well into the morning, I finally slept.

A few hours later I awoke to a typical windy March day. But this morning I felt different. Inside was a conviction that God was leading me in my search. I performed my morning chores quickly. Michael, now seven months old, took a morning nap after breakfast. I sent Sandy and Matt off to play and sat down at the kitchen table.

I bowed my head in prayer and thanksgiving before I solemnly, if not a little nervously, took the first Voice of Prophecy guide from the folder. After reading the introduction to myself, I then began to scan the questions along with the answers Dawn had penned straight from the Bible.

Suddenly I slammed it shut. *I must do this myself! I must find the answers in the Bible myself. I must see it in print, not my sister's handwriting.* Getting out the phone book, I found the number of the local Seventh-day Adventist church. The pastor answered the phone.

Pastor Burton and I talked for two hours that morning. He answered some of my questions and offered to bring me a series of Bible study guides called "The Bible Says." It, too, used only the Bible as a textbook, he said, and the lessons would lead me through the Bible a subject at a time.

"Do you have a Bible?" he asked.

"Yes, I do, but I'll have to find it."

The minister offered to bring the Bible lessons over that very afternoon. After we hung up I went in search of my Bible. It just *had* to be in the breezeway in all those boxes of books out there. I attacked the breezeway, determined to find my Bible. Although I searched for hours, stopping only briefly to tend to the needs of the children, I finally gave up from exhaustion. Ashamed and disgusted with myself, I phoned Pastor Burton. He offered to bring me an extra Bible that he had in his office.

That afternoon I answered the knock at my door to meet a middle-aged man of medium build wearing a light-blue suit. In his hand he carried a briefcase. Awkwardly I welcomed him in, and we both sat down. We talked for two hours.

Every question I gave him he answered confidently, saying, "Let's see what the Bible says about that." We looked up text after text together. I read each one as if for the very first time. They were all in perfect harmony. The Bible became more clear with each new text. It was like a blanket had been removed, revealing the secrets that had always been there. Pastor Burton sensed by my attitude that I was willing to believe anything he said, so he showed me a text, 1 Thessalonians 5:21: "Prove all things; hold fast that which is good."

"Don't take my word for it," he insisted. "Make me prove it from the Bible. If you do that you will always know that you are not being misled."

I openly asked him about the Catholic Church. "There are many fine brothers and sisters in all churches," he said. "God loves all His children, whatever church they are in, or even if they don't go to church at all."

Before he left Pastor Burton prayed with me. I hid the lessons and the Bible just before George came home. Although I felt guilty about keeping it from him, I knew he wouldn't understand.

The following afternoon I finished both lessons, eager to study the other 22 in the series. The pastor was pleasantly surprised when I called him to say that I needed more lessons. He offered to bring them the next morning.

The next day I rushed through the morning, tidying the house and feeding the kids. The pastor arrived as I was putting the last touches on the living room. He brought lessons 3 and 4. Again we studied together half the morning before he finally offered a prayer, inviting Sandy and Matt to join us.

Lesson 3 helped me to better understand the evil forces that rule our world—the forces that had murdered my children. I had never blamed God for killing them. But now, for the first time, I began to see the enormous part that Satan played in our lives.

Lesson 4 introduced me to Jesus, the Son of God, and His immense love for me and, more important, for my children. I learned of His compassion toward the weak and helpless and of His desire to make us whole and to bring us to Himself.

Whenever I had a question or could not find a text I would phone the pastor. Once I called and said meekly, "Pastor, this lesson says to look up 2 John. My Bible has only one John."

The pastor laughed sympathetically. "If you look at

the end of the New Testament, just before Revelation, you will find First, Second, and Third John. If it says just John, it means the Gospel of John toward the front of the New Testament."

Sure enough it was there.

Friday I phoned to ask about the services at the church on Saturday. I wanted to attend to see what it was like. Sabbath school would start at 9:30 a.m. followed by the church service at 11:00. The pastor said that he would not arrive until 11:00 because he had another service in a nearby town, but someone would greet me at the door.

The sun was just going down as we said goodbye.

"Happy Sabbath," Pastor Burton said in closing.

"I'll be there," I promised as I hung up the phone. I did not yet understand the full meaning of the Sabbath.

That evening I vowed to bring myself out of hiding. I told my husband about the lessons I was doing. He became angry.

"I thought we agreed that you were going to take some Catholic lessons."

"I was going to, George. But I prayed about it all night the night we talked, and these lessons are really good and I am going to do them. And I'm going to take Sandy and Matt to Sabbath school in the morning. I'll leave Michael here because 9:30 is his nap time."

"Sabbath school?" he questioned sarcastically.

"Yes. Dawn goes, and she says Darcy has a great time. It will be good for Sandy and Matt."

Angry that I had made my decision without consulting him, he stood silently. What was I getting his kids into?

"Don't you dare leave them, Joy. I want you to stay with them all the time."

"I will! I'll sit right with them," I promised.

"You'd better. They've never been left before. Don't you dare leave them."

My husband was extremely unhappy when he went to bed that night. Feeling that he was losing a part of me, he slept restlessly, wrestling with his thoughts.

My first Sabbath was cold and raining. As I dressed Sandy and Matt for church I avoided George. But I was excited for the children. I knew they would enjoy being with the other children in a structured atmosphere. I nursed Michael and fixed a bottle of juice for George to give him when he woke from his nap. Our kiss was strained as I said goodbye at the door. I hated hurting him.

Sandy talked all the way to the little church. We turned on Laramie Street and searched until we came to a tall old white building with a sign that read: "Seventh-day Adventist Church, Pastor Wilbur Burton."

*Wilbur*, I thought. *That was Grandpa's name. I'll have to tell the pastor about that.*

A young Asian man met us at the door. "Are you Joy?" he asked.

"Yes," I said.

"The cradle roll is down the hall. If you would like to go on into the sanctuary I will take the children down."

"No, I have to stay with them," I apologized. "They've never been left before."

The three of us followed him down the hall. The room was bright with pint-sized chairs, pictures of Jesus, and handmade crafts. A dozen children played quietly, awaiting the time to begin. Two women supervised their play. They welcomed us and invited Sandy and Matt to choose a chair. Matt was a little frightened and decided that Mommy's lap was the best place to be. Two other mothers stayed to be with their little ones.

Sabbath school was great fun. Sandy especially liked "The Raindrops Fall With a Pitter-Patter-Pat" song. She enjoyed putting felts on the board. Matt was more content to be a spectator.

After Sabbath school we all went to the drinking fountain before church began, then sat in a pew toward the front of the sanctuary. The Asian man introduced me to his wife and his 2-year-old daughter, Elizabeth, who had been in Sabbath school with us earlier.

The music began as the pastor and two elders entered. His eyes lit up when he saw me smiling happily. He welcomed each visitor by name in his opening words. I glowed with warmth, feeling truly welcome.

To my surprise after the opening song and the announcements he called out, "Children, it's story time!"

Every child in the sanctuary came hurrying up to the front and sat before the pastor's wife, who coaxed Sandy and Matt to join them. She was a kind, loving woman and a terrific storyteller. The children sat, mouths gaping, as she told her story. I looked around to find that the adults, too, were listening and enjoying it.

When the story ended the children quietly returned to their parents. After the sermon we all stood for the closing song, but I didn't hear the page number, and I had left my program in the Sabbath school room. Frantically I tried to find the song. Pastor Burton stepped down, placed his hymnal in my hands, and took mine back to the pulpit, never missing a note.

A potluck dinner was served after church, but I had to decline. Michael was surely awake and would want to nurse when I got home. Besides, I didn't want to press George. I took home with me two more Bible lessons.

George and I talked little the rest of the day. I spent part of the afternoon reading the children's Sabbath school magazine to the kids. That night before I put them to bed I taught them how to pray.

# THIRTEEN

# I WILL SEE THEM AGAIN!

During the next week I tried to avoid any confrontations with George. He played with the kids so he would not have to talk with me. I did my lessons during the day and hid them before he returned home. Pastor Burton came by with two more lessons on Thursday.

I took Sandy and Matt to church again the next Sabbath. Sandy recited her memory verse all by herself, and Matt decided it was safe to leave my lap and put felts on the felt board. I brought home two more lessons. George had made it clear that he didn't like the pastor visiting while he was not home. Of course, he wasn't welcome in the evenings either. Because of this, we kept in touch by phone through the week.

Finally I decided to bring the lessons into the open. I wanted so much to share them with my husband. If he could only see what I had, he would know, he would understand. This time I did not put them away. When he arrived home to find me working on one of them, his face dropped in disgust. "You're not even trying to hide them," he said angrily as he slammed the front door.

Speechless, I lowered my head to avoid his eyes.

"Can't you answer me!" he demanded.

I shook my head.

As he stomped angrily into the bedroom to change his clothes, I quietly folded the lesson sheet and went into the kitchen to start dinner.

George and I had always agreed on everything—or at least we could each bend a little to see the other's point of view. We had always shared the same goals and dreams and priorities. Why couldn't we share our faith in God?

I had never thought anything would come between us—certainly not the Bible! "I must stand my ground, though," I decided. "I have a right to seek God in the way I feel is right. I must not back down."

After dinner I brought out the lesson again and sat in the living room to finish it. Although George never said a word, he was visibly upset.

The following evening I was reading a book called *The Great Controversy* when he walked in the door. Exploding into a rage, he slammed the door so hard I thought it would fall off its hinges.

"You're not going to do this, Joy!" he yelled. "I've given it a lot of thought, and you are going to stop all of this! You are my wife, and we are a family. If you want to go to church, we are Catholics. I didn't make you join. You wanted to. You made that decision yourself. Now, I'm the head of this house, and I'm going to start acting like it. Do you understand?" He shook his finger at me.

For the first time I was afraid of him, of what he might do, but my stubborn spirit would not let me back down. He had taken his stand. Now I must make mine.

"George, I have a right to study the Bible and read

whatever I want. It's a free country. I have never gone against you and I love you and I want us to be a family. I'm sorry this hurts you so badly. I don't want to hurt you. But I must do this, and you have no right to stop me. All I want is to learn the truth and see the kids again. Why can't you understand that?"

We kept apart throughout the evening. That night I cried myself to sleep as George slept with his back to me. I wouldn't have even been doing all this if the kids hadn't been killed. I was doing it because I needed them back more than anything in the world. Was I going to lose George in the process? Why, God? George and I had comforted each other during the worst of times. Why were we fighting so venomously five years later?

During the next several weeks he began to quietly resign himself to my strong will. In return, I did the lessons only when he was gone and only occasionally read a religious book in front of him. It attracted less attention.

The pastor gave me some old magazines called *Signs of the Times,* and to my surprise George actually flipped through one, even scanning an article or two.

Finally I reached the lessons on the subject that I wanted to know most about. I had already deluged the pastor with questions about death and heaven and Christ's return. He had whetted my appetite, but promised that the lessons would fulfill my need to know when I reached that point. And now I was there.

As I opened the lesson about death I felt as if I had been handed a golden key to a special secret box.

"The living know that they shall die: but the dead know not any thing, neither have they any more a reward; for the memory of them is forgotten. Also their love, and their hatred, and their envy, is now perished; neither have they any more a portion for ever in any thing that is done under the sun" (Ecclesiastes 9:5, 6).

"There is no work, nor device, nor knowledge, nor wisdom, in the grave, whither thou goest" (verse 10).

These and other texts offered written proof that my children were really dead. They had not sprouted wings and become angels or floated around ghostlike, as bodiless spirits. Nor were they in a place called limbo, searching for more knowledge, or suffering torments in hell. My children had not been reincarnated into some other person. Instead, they were asleep, unconscious.

If the truth were to stop here, though, I would still have no hope of seeing my children again. Death would be the final end. But the truth goes on to a beautiful finish: "For God so loved the world, that he gave his only begotten Son, that whosoever believeth in him should not perish, but have everlasting life" (John 3:16).

A ray of hope shone through those words. Death is truly an enemy—an enemy that Jesus Christ conquered when He died for us all upon the cross. Christ chose to leave heaven to save humanity. Living a human existence and setting a perfect example for us to follow, He chose to die that we might live. Winning the victory over death, He ascended into heaven alive.

But before He went He made a promise: "In my

Father's house are many mansions: if it were not so, I would have told you. I go to prepare a place for you. And if I go and prepare a place for you, I will come again, and receive you unto myself; that where I am, there ye may be also" (John 14:2, 3).

When Jesus ascended toward heaven, a cloud of angels received Him. As the disciples watched, two angels stood by them and declared, "Ye men of Galilee, why stand ye gazing up into heaven? this same Jesus, which is taken up from you into heaven, shall so come in like manner as ye have seen him go into heaven" (Acts 1:11).

He promised He would come back again, to take us home with Him. "Marvel not at this: for the hour is coming, in which all that are in the graves shall hear his voice, and shall come forth" (John 5:28, 29).

"The Lord himself shall descend from heaven with a shout, with the voice of the archangel, and with the trumpet of God: and the dead in Christ shall rise first: Then we which are alive and remain shall be caught up together with them in the clouds, to meet the Lord in the air: and so shall we ever be with the Lord" (1 Thessalonians 4:16, 17).

At last I had found my answer! My children had not been reincarnated into some other person with new parents, as Mom had told me. They were not burning in hell, nor were they in a place called limbo. They were asleep, waiting for Jesus to come.

A popular belief today is that the dead go to heaven as soon as they die to live in eternal bliss. They can even look down and see what is happening here on earth. But how could my kids be truly happy if they were able to see all the tears that I had shed for them?

Once, when Tonya was barely 3, I fell into a state of depression. George had been working long hours, leaving me at home with all the kids and no car. That day it got the best of me. I lay across the bed, sobbing in despair. Tonya came in and patted me on the back. "What's wrong, Mommy?" she asked.

"Oh, Baby, I just want Daddy to come home," I cried.

Tonya wrapped her arms around me. "I'm Daddy, Mommy," she comforted. "I'm Daddy."

Tonya wanted more than anything to help Mommy stop crying, even if that meant becoming Daddy! How, then, could my daughter be happy in heaven, seeing the pain and loneliness I had suffered since her death? All she would want would be to come back down to earth so that Mommy wouldn't cry anymore. Would heaven really be paradise to her?

Another sober reality also became plain to me. When I was a child of about 12 or 13 a group of us kids started dabbling in spiritism. We even had séances and tried calling up the spirits of the dead. Some very unusual things happened that could only have been the result of a supernatural power. Fortunately, we escaped this trap. But I've read about spiritism since, and I now realize the danger that we were in and how the Bible teaching about life after death guards a person against that threat. If people who die are truly dead in every sense, unconscious in the grave until Jesus comes, then there is no way that they can return to talk to us.

What really frightened me was the book that I received from a man in Chicago called *Life After Life,* though I am sure that he meant well in sending it. It told of people who had apparently died on the operating table and been brought back to life. Such individuals claimed that their souls had separated from their bodies and that they could look down on their bodies lying on the operating table with the doctors working over them. They all observed a beautiful light, which some described as God or Jesus, while others claimed that it radiated with love and drew them toward it.

Many said that they saw loved ones who had died coming to greet them. Once they revived, they no longer feared death. Most felt that they had been on their way to heaven.

But if the Bible is true, then whatever these people experienced, it could not have been contact with their loved ones who had passed away, for those loved ones are now dead.

Most Christians reject the blatant spiritism that my friends and I got caught up in for a brief time when I was a child. My fear, however, is that Christian people who misunderstand the Bible's teaching about life after death will be deceived by this "life after life" idea into a subtle form of spiritism without even realizing it.

God has many children asleep in the graves—children who would not be dead were it not for Satan's tempting lies. God wants them to live again. That is why He sent His Son to win the victory over death.

For thousands of years God's people waited for His first coming. Today we look for His second coming. The promise is sure, for God does not lie. And when He returns, He will take us home.

"God shall wipe away all tears from their eyes; and there shall be no more death, neither sorrow, nor crying, neither shall there be any more pain: for the former things are passed away" (Revelation 21:4).

The former things, the wicked, the evil, will pass away. So many times people have tried to blame God for the loss of their loved ones. When a singer dies they say, "Perhaps God needed a good singer in heaven."

If God had meant for my children to die, how can we punish the murderers for fulfilling God's plan?

But someday soon Jesus will return to restore the earth and do away with the evil ones of this world. They will burn just as the tares at the time of harvest in Jesus' parable (Matthew 13:24–30). A cleansing fire will destroy all the impurities of our present world, taking all the evil ones with it.

For the first time I began to feel sorry for the two responsible for my children's deaths. For today I began to look for a blessed hope, a sure promise. Someday my kids will be raised to life. If I am alive I will be there to see it and I will be caught up to meet them in the air.

Someday we can be a family again, and nothing bad will ever happen again—never.

But for the murderers there is only death. Permanent death, for they will be gathered as tares and burned till there is nothing left to feed the flames.

For the first time since the kids were killed I felt satisfied with the answer. I only regretted that it took so long to find it. Once I knew the truth no other explanation made any sense. Dawn was right. If when you die you go straight to heaven, why is Jesus coming back?

A certain happiness and assuredness filled my heart. A burden lifted from me that I had carried far too long. I could actually read the Bible and understand its meaning. I now knew what kind of God I served. He was truly almighty and all loving. I really think that He, too, cried when my children were killed. He loved them as much as I did. I could do nothing to save them. God could. And He did. He sent His Son.

# FOURTEEEN

# BACK TO THE OZARKS

George decided it was time to return to the Ozarks. We spent hours scanning books and magazines on homesteading. Buying a pop-up camper, we readied it for our journey. It was to be our "Conestoga wagon," in which we would live until we bought a piece of land. The pop-up would give us the freedom to search out the right town without the worry of renting a house until we were ready.

Carefully we listed the items we should take with us. Space would be a big concern. Only the necessities and a few toys would make the trip. Everything else would go into storage.

The journey excited me. George and I had begun to talk again. A whole new adventure was beginning to take shape. A common goal was about to become a reality. The plans alone had brought us back to the old familiar closeness we had known before. Still, I worked diligently to finish the last of the lessons. I was determined to get them done before we left town.

I learned that Seventh-day Adventists have one of the largest religious school systems in the country. Once George and I had wanted the kids to go to Catholic schools. Now I hoped to have them attend Adventist schools. My husband was against it, but it didn't matter yet. None of them would be ready for school for several more years. However, I did want to settle in a town that had an Adventist church. Pastor Burton gave me a list of the Ozarks towns that had churches and schools. If I had anything to say about our destination, we would end up in one of them.

By the end of April I was flying through the last of the lessons. I absorbed them quickly, my new knowledge making me more confident about my life than I had ever dreamed. George accepted my attending church with the kids, but I knew he hoped the move would bring an end to it all. It was only a few days away. We didn't know exactly when we would go, though we needed to leave at the first sign of spring in order to give us the entire summer and part of the fall to get a place before the cold weather set in again. I finished the last of my lessons and gave them to the pastor after church on the first day of May.

I knew we would be leaving before the middle of the month, but before we departed I desired to be baptized, to share in Christ's death and thus have a part in His resurrection. I had no idea where we were headed or what lay ahead for my family, but I wanted God to go with me. I knew I was ready to make that decision. Three others were scheduled to be baptized the very next Sabbath. I would join them.

My husband saw no sense in it at all. "You've already been baptized," he reasoned.

"But not by immersion," I explained. "I was only 12 years old when the Episcopal priest sprinkled my head. I didn't even know what it was for. Now I do, and I want to do it right this time."

"How many times do you have to be baptized?" he shot back.

"Only once. But George, I really want to do this. It means a lot to me."

For two days it bothered him.

"Is this a feather in the pastor's cap if he gets you in the tank?" he asked. "Is he afraid you'll leave town and he won't get credit for it?"

I ignored his sarcasm. My husband just didn't understand.

Monday he came home from work to announce that we were leaving first thing Thursday morning. He would start hauling boxes and furniture to the storage unit tomorrow. I did not question his motives, though I had an idea. We would leave two days before my planned baptism.

The next morning I helped George load the truck so he could run it to the storage unit. Most of the boxes had been leisurely packed during the previous weeks. Only the basics remained. The pop-up was already half-loaded with camping gear, and I had made duffle bags to hold our clothes. The kids had taken a few afternoon naps in the camper to familiarize themselves with it.

After George left I phoned Pastor Burton. I could not hold back the tears when I told him we were leaving Thursday morning and nothing would change my husband's mind. I was ready to go. Really I was. But I had so wanted to be baptized before I left. The pastor said he'd call me back the next day.

We whipped out a lot of loads that day, narrowing

what remained down to the necessities. Tomorrow we would pack up the last of the household items.

Pastor Burton called me Wednesday morning while George was at the storage unit.

"Guess what we're doing at the church?" he said.

"What?"

"We're filling the baptistry for you. You can be baptized tonight at 7:00 if you can come."

Having almost given up hope, I nearly burst with excitement. George would not be happy, but I was going to do it anyway.

That evening I went alone to the church, dressed in casual blue knit slacks and a pink silk blouse. I arrived to find that the whole congregation had come to share in my celebration. One of the women assisted me into the long weighted gown while the rest of the congregation sang a hymn.

As I stepped down into the baptismal waters to stand before the pastor, a wave of emotion flowed through me. The significance of the step I was about to take burst inside of me.

"I baptize thee in the name of the Father, and of the Son, and of the Holy Spirit," the pastor repeated as he placed a handkerchief over my face and lowered me gently into the water. A moment later I arose to a new life. I was a new person, reborn. The responsibility for keeping my baptismal vows would follow me the rest of my life. I had renounced the world and its sinful ways and had publicly accepted Jesus Christ as my personal Saviour and as the Saviour of my children also, for my own life seemed worthless without them. From this day forward, by the grace of God, I would keep the commandments and teach my children to do so. I would diligently watch for that wonderful day when Jesus would appear in the sky.

Quickly changing into dry clothes, I rejoined the congregation as they sang "The Old Rugged Cross." I stood before them, tears welling up in adoration as Elizabeth, the tiny Asian-American child, toddled toward me to place a beautiful white lily in my hand. Knowing I would miss these loving individuals, I could only pray that my journey would lead me to another congregation with people as beautiful as these.

George finished loading the storage unit the next morning while I made the final preparations on the camper. Carefully I placed my Bible, lessons, and a stack of religious magazines into a box and stored them under the dinette in the camper. I included a Bible storybook and some magazines for the kids. A final check of mandatory supplies, and we were on the road before noon. The trip was long, but the excitement of what lay ahead kept our spirits high.

Our first Ozark Sabbath morning was crisp. The sweet smell of the cedar trees and the sound of rushing water filled our senses. I held Sabbath school with the children in the open air, singing Jesus songs and reciting the children's memory verse. An elderly man passed us on his way to the river to fish. He smiled approvingly and winked at the children.

After lunch we put Michael in his baby backpack and hiked up one of the trails. This is where I belonged, among the trees, with the sky as my roof. I loved the woods, and I was happy that we had returned to the Ozarks.

We spent six weeks in state parks, cooking our evening meals on an open fire. After we washed the dishes in a pot of heated water, we would sit in lawn chairs and watch the flames as they flickered and danced. Michael would lie in his father's arms, listening to his heartbeat until sleep took over. He was quite a little camper at nine months.

Finally we bought a 10-acre parcel outside of Cassville, Missouri. The old house had burned to the ground nine years before, and the barn and chicken coop leaned precariously, but we were willing to gamble that the old well was good, and the site did have electricity. With a lot of hard work, it just might be home.

The local Seventh-day Adventist church was an old white structure, scarred by years of termite damage. But the people who filled it were kind and caring, and they openly welcomed the children and me. The small congregation had a surprisingly large number of infants and children, and an 83-year-old schoolteacher taught a class of 11 children from first to eighth grade in the basement of her home next door.

George took a job at one of the boat docks, which paid an all-time low in wages. He had to work Saturdays and Sundays, so Michael started going to Sabbath school with us. We were able to stay for the potluck dinners twice a month and even started singing at the nursing homes in town every other Sabbath after church. Friendships grew, and it wasn't long before everyone knew about the deaths of my other five. A few of the older children sensed my loss and became very close to me. Wherever I went, I seemed to gather the children about me.

Buying a screened tent, we set it up next to the camper to use as an outdoor kitchen. The flies and mosquitoes were terrible, and the summer heat bore down on us, forcing us to abandon the pop-up by 10:00 each morning. We stayed outside all day. Most days we went to a sand beach a few miles away to cool off in the lake. Sometimes we took along a bar of soap and bathed there. Soon we learned to take Ivory soap because it floats!

In the evenings we would sit in the screened tent and read by lantern light. George took an interest in the *Signs of the Times* magazines, and occasionally we even shared our opinions. But whenever I got too deep or serious, he would change the subject. I was thankful, though, that we were able to talk.

Eventually we had the electricity hooked up so we could use the lights in the camper and thus save on batteries. We all appreciated being able to run a fan during the night. It was stiflingly hot.

September 11, our wedding anniversary, saw us still camping on the property. The days had turned to Indian summer, and the nights were getting cold. Over an open fire I prepared a feast of fried chicken, rolls, and corn on the cob, then packed it all into a basket to take to the dock where George was working. We dined at a picnic table on the dock, customers and fellow workers joining us for a celebration toast afterward.

It was a simple, honest celebration, just as our lives had been all summer long. But the weather was changing, and we'd have to seek a more secure structure immediately.

After trading our pop-up camper for an 8' x 33' travel trailer, we hooked up a pump and pressure tank to the old well. To our relief, the water came out clear and sweet. We triple bunked the kids in the one bedroom, and George and I slept on a hide-a-bed couch in the tiny living area.

The top students from each of the Adventist church schools in Missouri were invited to attend a weeklong camp and to tour the Missouri State Penitentiary. Two of my favorite girls won the honor in our tiny school. Pastor Ron Atkinson and his wife took them in their camper. They knew that the two boys who had killed my kids were in that prison. I was curious to know what the daily life of the prisoners was like and told the pastor that I wanted to talk to them about it when they returned.

During the tour a student from another area asked, "Who was the youngest prisoner ever to come here?"

"His name is Billy Dyer," the tour guide told them. "He arrived here at the age of 15. Serving consecutive life sentences for the shooting deaths of four children, he has been in solitary confinement since he arrived here. He eats alone, and he is escorted alone to shower and to exercise. We have to keep him in confinement because the other prisoners would probably kill him if we put him in with the general prison population. His accomplice, Ray Richardson, was in solitary the entire time he served here. But he was paroled his first time up."

The shock of learning that Richardson had been out quite some time really hit me hard. It had been only six years since he had helped Billy kill my kids. The pain of losing them was still fresh in my memory. My emotions were all confused. I really didn't know how to feel.

On the one hand, as a Christian, I did feel sorry for Billy and Ray, because I knew that the final judgment would fall on them some day too. I did not envy them. The death they had inflicted upon my children was only temporary, for my children would live again. But the death that would fall on these two killers would be total, permanent destruction.

I also realized—and it took a long time to accept—that if Billy and Ray were truly, heart-wrenchingly sorry for what they had done, God would forgive them too. After all, we are all human, we all make mistakes, and we all have a right to forgiveness when we repent. I have done things in my own life that I am not proud of, and I am confident that God has forgiven me. My past mistakes didn't keep me from being a potentially good person later in life. I am a Christian now. Billy and Ray have a right to that transformation too.

On the other hand, there have been times when I could not control my feelings of rage and anger for what they did to my family. They had irreversibly altered our lives forever. I was supposed to hate the sin but love the sinner, and when I looked at the whole big picture I could. But when I focused on just me and how my children had suffered under their hands, my hate for them was intense.

I hadn't wanted Ray to be paroled that soon—I wanted him to be properly punished for his role in the crime, and I didn't feel that he had been. He was free to marry, to raise a family, to be a grandpa some day—all things that my kids could never do because of the crime committed by his hand. Yes, I could accept his repentance and God's forgiveness. But I had a really rough time coping with the fact that he could live a normal life after depriving my children of doing so, and so soon

A few weeks later Pastor Atkinson's daughter died in an auto accident, and the pastor and his wife drove to Illinois for the funeral. The next Sabbath morning I watched a film about prison reform shown during Sabbath school. The film told about the Christian ministries conducted in prisons around the country and their effects on the inmates there. Throughout the film I kept thinking of Billy and Ray.

Had they changed? Were they sorry for what they had done, or were they tough punks now? Did they have nightmares reliving what they had done, or were they totally insensitive to their crime? Had they, or would they, find Christ? Did I really want them to?

The film interviewed an inmate, one of the Charles Manson family involved in the Sharon Tate killings. He said he was sorry for what he had done and hurt for the family members of those he had killed. If there was anything he could do to bring them back, he declared, he would do it, even if he himself had to die. But he couldn't change things.

As I listened I started hyperventilating. My body and face felt numb as my emotions raged inside of me. I couldn't unscramble my Christian feelings from my selfish human ones. Did Billy feel this way too?

The film ended, and I turned to some friends for comfort. Sobbing, I explained my reaction to them. I didn't want to hate Billy and Ray! Jesus didn't hate anybody. How could I call myself a Christian and still hate? With time and love and information, anybody could become a good person. But how could I possibly love these two after what they had done to my babies? How in the world was I supposed to feel?

My friends calmed me down. They told me it was all right to feel anger at what had happened to my children. And they cried with me, giving me strength and planting the seed that would become this book.

"Joy, have you ever considered writing about your experience?" one of the women asked. "You know, Mrs. Atkinson really admires you for your strength. She may need you when they get back from the funeral in Illinois. You know what it's like to lose a child."

We talked for quite a while. *Maybe a book would be good,* I thought. It would be a way to reach a lot of people, to share my loss, and my victory. Perhaps it would bring hope to others who had lost someone close to them. I decided that if God really wanted me to write a book, He would help me with the words. I started the very next day.

It was easy at first, recalling my love for my children

and the wonderful things they did. But as the time drew closer to write about Stephanie's illness and the children's deaths, I discovered that I could not express my true feelings without throwing myself back to that time. I relived it all over again. Unable to even set my feelings aside to fix dinner, I carried them with me everywhere. Affecting how I treated my family and friends, they left me depressed and short-tempered.

When I wrote about the time when I didn't know Christ and was searching for answers, I even became angry with God. I became so absorbed in reliving the experience that I even failed to realize that now I *did* know and that I should be at peace. The first time I tried to write about the murders it affected me so much that I had to put the whole project on hold for several months for the sake of my family. The turmoil I relived when I finally did write it was tremendous. It was a difficult time for me, but my friends at the church, and a neighbor, supported my efforts and kept me going.

# AND THE GRAVES SHALL BE OPENED

We lived the entire winter in our travel trailer. By early May it had been one year since we'd left on our unknown journey. For one whole year we had camped—had dared to do something that most right-minded people would never even consider. A whole year without a house. Our children had celebrated their first, third, and fifth birthdays in a pop-up camper! But they were healthy and robust.

We had no money for the home we had come to build. Our dream was not materializing here. George's knee required surgery, the result of an old injury that was constantly causing trouble and promised only to get worse unless it received immediate attention. We sold the land and moved to Springfield to be near a big hospital. For the next six months George was out of work, recuperating from the surgery, regaining strength in his knee.

His convalescence finally over, we decided to take an extended vacation to see the Rocky Mountains. It was late October when we headed out with all our camping gear in the back of our pickup truck.

The Rockies were more magnificent than we ever imagined. They gave a whole new meaning to the word *awesome*. At times the scenery was so beautiful that we didn't know which way to look first. We "oohed" and "aahed" for miles.

For two weeks we traveled from town to town, taking notes, and exploring. We'd found a whole new playground. Although we loved the Ozarks, they had only taken from us. Always we had gone down there with our hopes high, only to leave penniless. Perhaps we could make our dream come true in the Rockies.

Hurrying back to Springfield, we packed our things and moved to Kansas. We were going to do it right this time. George enrolled in a one-year course in the auto mechanics field at a vo-tech school. He hoped that the training would enable us to move to the mountains in style.

The local Adventist church was old and in desperate need of paint. The congregation was tiny and consisted mostly of retired people. They had no children's Sabbath school department, so I volunteered to be the teacher. My first Sabbath there I carted home boxes of felts and other visual aids so that I could familiarize myself with the materials I had to work with and organize the mess that had lain dormant for years. The next Sabbath I was ready with a program for the children—all five of them.

I poured myself into the church, cleaning, organizing, decorating, picking dandelions in the yard on lazy summer days. "Recognize a need and fill it" was my new motto. If it needed to be done, you could count on Joy to do it. The congregation loved my energy and creativity. I could take nothing and turn it into something useful. I brought life into the group. It felt good to be so important a part of this little congregation.

At the same time I wanted with all my heart for George to see what I experienced. He now accepted my constant involvement with the church and even agreed that our children could attend Adventist schools. My husband had come a long way since I had begun the lessons in Manhattan, Kansas. As long as he had breath in his lungs, there was hope that he would also someday discover what I had found. It was my constant prayer.

George met Pastor Thurber, a young man with carefree hair and a full mustache. The two of them related well. They shared common interests in nature, camping, canoeing, and each had a military background full of stories to swap. My husband adored Pastor Thurber's baby daughter Kristy.

Soon George got involved with our church group, joining us for a Father's Day dinner at a local pizza shop, the pastor's surprise birthday party, and a weekend at an Adventist summer camp outside of Boulder, Colorado, where we canoed, rode horses, hiked, and popped popcorn over the fire. When a Revelation seminar started I begged George to attend with me. I had passed up two of them in previous towns, and I really did want to go. It was to run three evenings a week for eight weeks. He gave in, and we went together. As it turned out, he began to enjoy going, though it was difficult for him to study engines all day and God all evening.

We did our lessons together before each meeting, he looking up the answers in the Bible so I could write them down. It was wonderful to see him reading from the Bible. Two years before we had fought over it. Now we were sharing it, as it should be. Christ was tapping on his shoulder, and in his own way my husband was responding.

George still looked longingly at the Catholic Church. He missed the stained-glass windows and the rhythmic beauty of the mass. I understood how he felt. The Catholic Church is full of wonderful, caring people. I would never forget the Maddens and the rest of the neighborhood back in Kansas City. They had done so much for me. Their children were all good, respectful Christians, exactly what I wanted my children to be. But I had learned things that would not allow me to be a Catholic anymore. I really think George understood that too.

My involvement in the church made the year go quickly. George had a perfect attendance record at school, and he'd kept his grades high. A few weeks before graduation we took a trip to the mountains to scout out some employment. He landed a job in the parts department of an automobile dealership and we returned to Kansas just long enough to pack.

Since then we have lived in a small community in the Rocky Mountains. I became the children's Sabbath school teacher and active in my local church. I've changed since I became a Seventh-day Adventist. And yet I am still the same. I carry a hope within me that very soon my Saviour will return to carry me home and to restore my children back to life.

Sandy, Matt, and Michael came to know something that the other five never had a chance to experience.

They learned that in all they did an angel watched over them. On a trip once to visit Grandma Swift we encountered a positively brilliant sunset. The colors that splashed out from around the clouds were truly magnificent. Michael jumped up from the back seat and thrust his tiny finger toward the sky, his face alive with excitement.

"Look, Mommy!" he cried. "Jesus is coming!"

The adrenalin began to pump inside me at the thought of such a sight. Imagine it. The King Himself sitting on that cloud! I looked deep into the face of my 3-year-old son. He was just a baby, and yet he carried a hope inside him that was almost as strong as mine.

They never met their brothers and sisters, yet through stories and pictures they know them almost as well as they know Jesus Christ. They look forward to that wonderful reunion day when they can finally meet the siblings they should have spent a lifetime playing with. I, too, await that day with great anticipation.

At one time I felt inadequate, that perhaps my faith wasn't strong enough to carry me through those moments when my grief or anger got the best of me. But the Bible introduced me to Job, a man of great faith who loved and obeyed God all his life. When Satan began to slowly take away all that he had, Job's feelings of grief and despair were immense. He wanted to die, but he lived to rise above it, and his faith in God was restored.

Peter, the disciple of Christ, wanted more than

anything to follow His perfect example. And yet so many times he failed. His feelings of inadequacy bore down on him more than once.

Although men of God, they still experienced times of great mental anguish. I, too, am Job. And I am Peter. I now walk with confidence, for I know that when my Father looks at me He sees the perfection of His Son.

Although it has been a quarter century since I last saw my children alive, they are still daily in my thoughts, though they now reside in the back of my memory, giving my three living children priority. Still, everything I do for these three, all my thoughts about how I want them to grow up, my entire attitude about them, is directly tied to what happened to the other five.

We still tell Sandy, Matt, and Michael stories about their brothers and sisters. They feel honored when we entrust them with something that was once their brother's or sister's, and they seem to be proud when we find something about them that was like one of the others.

I still dream about what it would be like if we were all together. I dream of an enormous country home with enough bedrooms to handle a family of 10. I see big pots simmering on the kitchen stove, full of chilis and stews. And I have solemnly acknowledged each birthday, acutely aware that I have lost yet another year of watching their lives.

I still cry for them, wanting them to run up and hug me once more. They say that time heals all wounds, but a wound this deep does not heal. It only scars over, the scab coming loose from time to time, allowing the wound to bleed all over again. There still come moments when my grief is unbearable, and the tears roll in torrents down my cheeks like water from a broken dam.

But they do not feel my tears, for they are sleeping. They are not aware that I often still speak of them, recalling the things that they did when they were here. They're not aware of the years that have passed since their last breath. They're not aware of the hours I spend each day lost in my memories, or the fear I carry that those memories may someday begin to fade. Nor do they have any idea how much I miss them and long to be with them.

Yet I am at peace, for I realize that my Father has already arranged for me to be with them again. So I must wait.

But one day soon the sky will fill with brightness, and a cloud will appear that everyone shall see. A cloud of angels. Tens of thousands of them. And amid them will sit the Son of Man, Jesus Christ, wearing a crown and carrying a sickle. For it is time to harvest the earth.

And the trumpet shall sound. And in that moment, that glorious moment, the ground shall tremble. And the graves shall be opened. Praise God!